Saturday Night at Old Smokey

A Poignant Comedy with Music by
Ron Osborne

Musical arrangements by
Steve Sensenig

A SAMUEL FRENCH ACTING EDITION

SAMUELFRENCH.COM

Copyright © 2012 by Ron Osborne

ALL RIGHTS RESERVED

Cover art designed by Gene Weber, Weber Graphic Design, LLC © 2011
(webergraphicdesign.com)

CAUTION: Professionals and amateurs are hereby warned that *SATURDAY NIGHT AT OLD SMOKEY* is subject to a Licensing Fee. It is fully protected under the copyright laws of the United States of America, the British Commonwealth, including Canada, and all other countries of the Copyright Union. All rights, including professional, amateur, motion picture, recitation, lecturing, public reading, radio broadcasting, television and the rights of translation into foreign languages are strictly reserved. In its present form the play is dedicated to the reading public only.

The amateur/professional live stage performance rights to *SATURDAY NIGHT AT OLD SMOKEY* are controlled exclusively by Samuel French, Inc., and licensing arrangements and performance licenses must be secured well in advance of presentation. PLEASE NOTE that amateur Licensing Fees are set upon application in accordance with your producing circumstances. When applying for a licensing quotation and a performance license please give us the number of performances intended, dates of production, your seating capacity and admission fee. Licensing Fees are payable one week before the opening performance of the play to Samuel French, Inc., at 45 W. 25th Street, New York, NY 10010.

Licensing Fee of the required amount must be paid whether the play is presented for charity or gain and whether or not admission is charged.

Stock/professional licensing fees quoted upon application to Samuel French, Inc.

For all other rights than those stipulated above, apply to: Samuel French, Inc., 45 West 25th Street, New York, NY 10010.

Particular emphasis is laid on the question of amateur or professional readings, permission and terms for which must be secured in writing from Samuel French, Inc.

Copying from this book in whole or in part is strictly forbidden by law, and the right of performance is not transferable.

Whenever the play is produced the following notice must appear on all programs, printing and advertising for the play: "Produced by special arrangement with Samuel French, Inc."

Due authorship credit must be given on all programs, printing and advertising for the play.

ISBN 978-0-573-70013-2

No one shall commit or authorize any act or omission by which the copyright of, or the right to copyright, this play may be impaired.

No one shall make any changes in this play for the purpose of production.

Publication of this play does not imply availability for performance. Both amateurs and professionals considering a production are strongly advised in their own interests to apply to Samuel French, Inc., for written permission before starting rehearsals, advertising, or booking a theatre.

No part of this book may be reproduced, stored in a retrieval system, or transmitted in any form, by any means, now known or yet to be invented, including mechanical, electronic, photocopying, recording, videotaping, or otherwise, without the prior written permission of the publisher.

RENTAL MATERIALS

An orchestration consisting of **Lead Sheets** will be loaned two months prior to the production ONLY on the receipt of the Licensing Fee quoted for all performances, the rental fee and a refundable deposit.

Please contact Samuel French for perusal of the music materials as well as a performance license application.

IMPORTANT BILLING AND CREDIT REQUIREMENTS

SATURDAY NIGHT AT OLD SMOKEY must give credit to the Author of the Play in all programs distributed in connection with performances of the Play, and in all instances in which the title of the Play appears for the purposes of advertising, publicizing or otherwise exploiting the Play and/or a production. The name of the Author *must* appear on a separate line on which no other name appears, immediately following the title and *must* appear in size of type not less than fifty percent of the size of the title type.

In addition the following credit *must* be given in all programs and publicity information distributed in association with this piece:

First produced by Barter Theatre
Abingdon, Virginia
by Richard Rose, Producing Artistic Director

Cover art designed by Gene Weber, Weber Graphic Design, LLC © 2011
(webergraphicdesign.com)

SATURDAY NIGHT AT OLD SMOKEY (then titled *Saving Old Smokey*) premiered on the main stage of Barter Theatre, the LORT-member State Theatre of Virginia (Richard Rose, Producing Artistic Director) in Abingdon, Virginia on June 9, 2011 through August 13, 2011. Mary Lucy Bivins directed. The set designer was Cheri Prough DeVol; costume designer was Liz Whittemore; sound design was by Bobby Beck; lighting designer was Michael Barnett; stage manager was Seymour; and the music director was Steve Sensensig. The cast was as follows:

EMMA	Marnee Hollis
JINKS	Tricia Matthews
OLIVE	Erin Parker
CORDELIA	Ashlie Roberson
TAMMY	Ashley Campos
HOWARD	Rick McVey

CHARACTERS

EMMA – A caring mother on a mission to preserve a treasure, 50.

JINKS – Emma's creative friend who's at war with everything Southern, 50 or so.

OLIVE – Another friend whose love of the South conflicts with Jinks, also 50 or so.

CORDELIA – An ambitious, talented, take-charge young lady engaged to Emma's son, 20ish.

TAMMY – Howard's attractive companion with a dream, 20 to 30.

HOWARD – A pompous stranger with multiple secrets, 40 to 60.

SETTING

All action takes place in "Old Smokey Country Store," a small, family-owned general store situated on the crest of the highest mountain in the county. The store is from another time. It consists of one large room featuring shelves, a checkout counter (on which there's a table-top radio), as well as a chair or two and perhaps an old pot-belly stove. (Note: Because the store is in the process of being reopened, shelves and walls – except for decorative signs, etc. – are bare at the beginning of the play; a few items of merchandise – as suggested in the script – are added as the play develops.) A door to the rear leads to a second entrance/exit; another at stage left opens to an unseen office/store room. Importantly, there's a porch at the front of the set, along with steps which lead from a parking lot to the area that forms the porch and, behind it, the aforementioned sales area. Some of the characters who visit Old Smokey access it via the theatre aisles and down center, a.k.a., the store's parking lot. There should be no doubt that the view from that porch makes any journey to Old Smokey worth the trip.

TIME

The mountains of east Tennessee, early spring, present.

AUTHOR'S NOTES

For purposes of this play, Old Smokey Country Store functions as an allegorical character, representing the past (when traditional values, including family and friendships, seemed to rule) as well as the future (it's Teddy's dream and his best chance for recovery). It is into this environment that the play's characters enter...several seeking new adventures; one representing the greed and celebrity of the moment, another yearning to preserve the values that helped build Old Smokey.

The script may suggest that the characters Jinks and Olive dislike one another. That's not the case, and the actors should avoid giving that impression. The fact is these small town women have a deep-seated affection for each other, if only because they enjoy the competitive verbal jostling their association provides.

The play features more than a dozen old-time musical standards as well as traditional hymns and gospels. For a number of these, new lyrics replace those originally written for the music, creating humorous musical parodies that advance the plot. The actors portraying Emma, Cordelia, Jinks and Olive should have reasonably good singing voices. A Cordelia with guitar-playing skills would be a plus, although a tambourine or other hand-held percussion instrument could substitute for the guitar.

SCENES

ACT I

Scene 1 – Morning
Scene 2 – That evening
Scene 3 – The next afternoon
Scene 4 – Late afternoon, the following day

ACT II

Scene 1 – Moments after close of Act I
Scene 2 – An hour or so later
Scene 3 – Another hour or two later

SONGS/MUSIC

ACT I

Scene 2

This Little Light of Mine .... **TAMMY**

Scene 3

Way Up There .... **CORDELIA**
Old Smokey Country Store .... **CORDELIA & OLIVE**
Cumberland Gap .... **CORDELIA & EMMA**

Scene 4

Our Name is Old Smokey .... **CORDELIA & JINKS**

ACT II

Scene 2

We're Heading To Howard's Chicken .... **CORDELIA**

Scene 3

Oh, We're Live From Old Smokey, Yes We Are .... **CORDELIA, JINKS, OLIVE**
Down To The River To Pray .... **CORDELIA, EMMA, JINKS**
Go Tell It On The Mountain .... **CORDELIA & OLIVE**
Up On The Mountain Side .... **CORDELIA, EMMA & OLIVE**
Wabash Cannonball .... **CORDELIA & OLIVE**
Softly And Tenderly .... **OLIVE**
Hallelujah, We Shall Rise .... **CORDELIA, TAMMY, EMMA, OLIVE & JINKS**
Jordan Is A Hard Road To Travel .... **JINKS & OLIVE**
Dixie .... **OLIVE & JINKS**

All songs/music are in the public domain.

ACT ONE

Scene One

(The interior sales area of Old Smokey Country Store. In addition to a rear door and another leading to a side office/store room, we see several chairs as well as shelves that line the wall at stage left. The opposite wall features a counter [on which there's a radio] as well as additional shelves. Where wall space is available, there's an assortment of advertising memorabilia, perhaps including a sign reading, "You Want It, We Sell It" [followed by an illustration of crossed fingers]. In spite of the sign, it's obvious Old Smokey isn't ready for customers, if only because the store's shelves are empty. Nevertheless, there's a certain homey comfortableness about the space.)

*(**AT RISE**, the aforementioned is dark [we see only the area that leads to the store's porch and eventually to the inside sales area]. After a moment, a loud SHRIEK comes from inside Old Smokey. Immediately, **JINKS** – with bucket and mop in hand – enters from the rear of the theatre. She runs up an aisle as fast as her legs will carry her, shouting all the way.)*

JINKS. HOLD ON, EMMA! I'M COMING! BE THERE IN A MINUTE!

*(Lights up inside Old Smokey; we see **EMMA** who uses a broom to bat at something on the floor.)*

EMMA. *You*...get on out of here...! *(After a bit of a battle, she manages to open the rear door, sweep whatever startled her out.)* Go on...SCRAM!

JINKS. *(now alongside **EMMA**, excitedly)* What was it?

EMMA. If it was running around the restaurant you're about to open they'd close you down.

JINKS. Not if I caught it. Served it as my blue-plate special to good old Southerners...who'll eat anything...especially when ladled with salt and fried till Sunday.

EMMA. Why did I let it get like this? *(She uses her broom to clear a spider web.)*

JINKS. Because you've got a beauty shop to run. Not to mention...a number-one customer who needs a miracle Wednesdays at nine a.m.

EMMA. Old Smokey needs more than a miracle in a bottle –

JINKS. Yes. *(crosses to the porch, looks out)* But standing here... looking out...you can see all the way to tomorrow. Pretty as ever, huh?

(EMMA joins JINKS; both admire the stunning view as JINKS reconsiders what she's said.)

Of course...there's really nothing out there...except trees and –

EMMA. Don't start that.

JINKS. Which pretty much describes the South. Trees and weeds and –

EMMA. I love you to tears. But if you don't like it here, forget the restaurant –

JINKS. I'm about to teach folks here there's more to supper than fried chicken –

EMMA. Go somewhere you don't fuss about a dozen times a day.

JINKS. I don't know what you're talking about.

EMMA. Tell me one nice thing you've said about the South...*ever.*

JINKS. Well... *(She's deep in thought.)*

EMMA. I'm waiting...

JINKS. *(gleefully, perhaps clapping her hands)* It lost the Civil War.

EMMA. See what I mean?

JINKS. Imagine, Emma…a bunch of crazy Johnny Rebs running New York City. No *Lincoln* Center, no *Grant's* Tomb, no –

EMMA. *Yankee* Stadium. I understand, so stop!

JINKS. I'm here to help. *(begins to sweep the floor)*

EMMA. Good. Because I promised Teddy I'd have this place ready the minute he steps from the plane.

JINKS. He knows what you're planning?

EMMA. A month from today, this is my boy's place. Of course, it'll take him a while to get back to where he was.

JINKS. He's got you to help.

EMMA. And Cordelia.

JINKS. You think Cordelia's still an Old Smokey kind of gal – ?

EMMA. They're engaged!

JINKS. *(knows better than to question **CORDELIA**'s loyalty)* Of course, they are.

EMMA. It won't be easy for either of them. But he'll get better. Cordelia understands that. In the meantime –

JINKS. This is where Teddy needs to be.

EMMA. According to his doctors, it's the best medicine –

JINKS. *(takes **EMMA**'s hand, looking out, caringly with a smile in her voice)* The trees and the weeds –

EMMA. And the quiet and being someplace he loves after all he's been through. Plus, I'll have a man around to fix things his daddy never had the chance to do. And wouldn't you know…sitting empty all these years…a real estate agent called. He's got a buyer for this old place –

JINKS. You told him "no" –

EMMA. I told him my son has big plans for Old Smokey. Which don't include selling it anytime soon.

JINKS. Then let's get this place ready for new management.

(EMMA forces a smile. Silence as both women are busy sweeping. After a moment, the silence is broken by the DING-DING sound old-time service stations used to tell them there was a car at the pump. JINKS looks out.)

Look who's expecting somebody to pump gas in her gaudy red pickup...with that Stars and Bars *thing* plastered on the grill...currently flashing its red, white, and blue heart out?

(As EMMA looks out, we hear a vehicle AIR HORN. It plays the opening dozen notes of "Dixie.")

Ladies and Gentlemen...the Queen of the South *has* arrived!

EMMA. That pump's been dry for years. And don't start messing with her, especially that queen business... which she hates.

(OLIVE appears, then enters. JINKS greets her with an exaggerated Southern accent.)

JINKS. Ma'am. Can I fill it up for ya...?

OLIVE. At a dollar twenty-nine a gallon...*even you* can fill it up. You do know, Emma...you're selling your gas way too cheap?

JINKS. *(now sweetly with the same pronounced Southern accent)* Only to "friends" like you, Olive. No...no...let me say it the way folks in the *civilized* world say it... *(drops the accent, sounds like a Yankee)* Only to "friends" like you, Olive.

OLIVE. Oh, I do hope you'll talk like that all the time...*so nobody confuses you with one of us! (to* **EMMA***)* Speaking of being Southern and being proud of it!...driving up here I was rudely pulled over by an officer wanting to give me a ticket for some silly offense like "putting on mascara while driving." I'd have none of that, of course. So I asked myself what would catch this cute son-of-the south's attention. At which point I remembered my horn which I sounded and together we sang our little old national anthem. *(places her hand over her heart)*

EMMA. *(Unfortunately, she knows Olive's "national anthem.")* Dixie.

OLIVE. I ask you, Emma…who gives a ticket to a Southern belle who knows all *ten* verses?

JINKS. Even down here, things like that don't happen… right? *(looking hopefully at* **OLIVE***)*

OLIVE. *(smiling as she proudly sings or hums the following)* "I wish I was in the land of cotton" –

JINKS. *(to* **EMMA***)* What I said about folks like…you know who… *(smiles, points to* **OLIVE***)* I rest my case.

OLIVE. What does that mean?

EMMA. She's just playing with you again.

OLIVE. What she's doing is embarrassing herself again. Like she's embarrassing the whole town with that… butt-ugly sign outside her…so-called restaurant to be…that nobody in their right mind's gonna want to frequent…*ever*.

JINKS. And what's wrong with my sign?

OLIVE. *It's embarrassing!* Why, this morning I saw an out-of-state car pass by…the driver shaking his head like this year Christmas isn't coming. *It's giving the South a bad name!*

JINKS. *Hallelujah!*

OLIVE. If we have anything to be proud of – and obviously we've got lots to be proud of – it's our down-home cooking…*ESPECIALLY fried chicken!* So…for a Yankee to see a sign…*in Tennessee, of all places*…reading *"Fried-Free Zone Ahead"*…

EMMA. *(looking at* **JINKS**, *not wanting to believe it)* You didn't!

OLIVE. Carried by some...*fool*...marching around, *dressed in a crazy-looking chicken outfit...clucking and strutting like a two-hundred pound hen on steroids...*

*(***OLIVE** *demonstrates, folding her arms, moving them and her head up and down as she struts across the stage, making clucking sounds as she moves.* **EMMA** *observes; she's unhappy with both women.)*

JINKS. *(looking at* **EMMA**, *but pointing to* **OLIVE** *as she does her thing)* And who is the fool?

OLIVE. *Who was the two-hundred pound hen?*

EMMA. *What's wrong with the two of you?*

OLIVE. *She's* been mad at me for twenty-five years.

EMMA. You've been dear friends for twenty-five years.

OLIVE. You're forgetting. She was in love with my Jimmy! Oh, he was the man of her dreams. Except he wanted *me*. So we got married. Leaving somebody we know a fussy old maid...who dresses up in *fricken chicken outfits!*

JINKS. Well, he's yours now, sweetheart...*till death do you part*. Which should work out fine...considering *your* cute little old Jimmy Dunwitty is now our friendly neighborhood...*mortician.*

EMMA. Just leave...both of you. I'll do this by myself. *(picks up a broom, begins sweeping)*

OLIVE. I've come to help.

EMMA. The Lord knows I need help. But not from the two of you. At least not in the same room at the same time.

JINKS. I think maybe we can...*probably* get along...

OLIVE. This morning...*possibly.*

EMMA. What happened the last time the two of you had hair appointments the same morning?

(Silence as an embarrassed **OLIVE** *and* **JINKS** *look at the floor.)*

JINKS. It was an old mirror, Emma.

EMMA. And the water fight using my shampoo sprayers like AK-47s? With poor Henrietta Wiggins caught in the middle?

JINKS. I suppose she got a little wet –

EMMA. While learning a dozen words she'll never hear sitting in a Baptist Church. *(looks critically at* **OLIVE***)*

JINKS. In the interest of harmony...I'll admit...I started it.

OLIVE. That's a lie! *I started it!*

EMMA. It's hard to imagine...once upon a time you two were a singing duet on your way to the stage of the Grand Old Opry. Everybody said, "Oh, those 'Mountain Mamas'...they can sing like nobody's business. They will make East Tennessee proud!" And what have they become? Two *so-called "ladies"* who amuse themselves by fussing at one other at every opportunity!

JINKS. It's a small town, Emma.

OLIVE. I'm a walking, talking dust-buster. And Jinks, I hear, can sweep like nobody's business. Isn't that true... *(looking at* **JINKS***, forcing a smile, sweetly)* ...Jinks?

JINKS. On occasion, I can be a whiz with a broom... *(equally sweetly)* ...Olive.

OLIVE. And Cordelia will be helping tomorrow...when she gets off the air.

EMMA. Off the air?

OLIVE. I thought everybody knew.

JINKS. I've heard rumors...

OLIVE. I am here to confirm the wonderful news! Cordelia's got her own radio program. Of course, I keep telling her – with her considerable looks and musical talent – she ought to be on television. After all, she *did* win that big-time beauty pageant –

JINKS. Ah, yes. Our very own...Miss *Seedless* Watermelon of *Upper* Johnson County.

EMMA. She sang beautifully and looked even better. And we're *all* proud of her…! *(looking at* **JINKS** *critically)* Isn't that right, Jinks?

JINKS. Everybody knows I adore Cordelia.

OLIVE. Her program's called "Cordelia in the Mornin'." And it's something special…if I say so myself. Of course, I should say so. She *is* my daughter.

*(***EMMA** *and* **JINKS** *look at one another, not knowing what to make of it all.* **OLIVE** *notes their confusion.)*

If you don't believe me…listen.

*(***OLIVE** *steps to the table radio, turns it on. We hear a woman's voice.* **CORDELIA** *may be on the radio, but her broadcasting skills are being honed as we listen.)*

CORDELIA. *(radio voice)* Rusty's Auto, Truck, Motorcycle, Bicycle, Tricycle, and Lawnmower Emporium – where we're wheeling and dealing because wheels are our business – brings you the W-R-E-T…*We R East Tennessee*…ten a.m. news…brought to you this morning a few minutes after eleven…on everybody's favorite new county music program…*Cordelia in the Mornin'*…!"

OLIVE. All I can say is… *(with a mother's pride, applauding)* …look out, world…here comes Cordelia!

(Proud mama **OLIVE** *smiles broadly as a country song – playing on the radio – is up as the lights slowly dim to black. The music continues through the scene change.)*

End of Scene

Scene Two

(Old Smokey's front porch and a small portion of the adjoining parking lot, same day, late evening. **EMMA** *and her friends have left for the day, thus lights in the store are off.)*

*(**AT RISE**, the music we've heard through the scene change comes down gradually. It is dark, but not so dark that we can't see **TAMMY**, who approaches Old Smokey via an aisle, using a flashlight to find her way. We're about to learn she's an animated, splashy young woman [particularly in dress] as well as someone who's naive and not particularly well educated. What she lacks in intellect, however, she makes up for in looks, ambition and energy.)*

TAMMY. Howard. *(now using her flashlight to locate **HOWARD**)* Howard! Where are you?

*(**HOWARD**, a prosperous-looking fellow dressed in a coat and tie appears in an aisle; he walks backward toward the stage, all the time shining his flashlight into the dark. There's fear in his voice.)*

HOWARD. Did you see that?

TAMMY. What?

HOWARD. *The bear!*

TAMMY. A raccoon probably –

HOWARD. *It was a bear! It was huge! And it ran in front of me!*

TAMMY. Howard. It's okay if we're lost. 'Cause I get lost too. Especially when I decided I'd twiddled my thumbs in one place long enough. So, I packed my bag, drove till I didn't even know what state I was in…that's how lost *I* was. Howard, are you listening to me?

*(**HOWARD** ignores **TAMMY**, continues to use his flashlight to inspect the property.)*

TAMMY. Which is when I pulled over, got a job – if you call walking around with a coffee pot, saying, "Be right there, sugar" – a job. So I asked God to make things better. And, for a while they were...till it was the same old stuff all over again. *Except* I was alone. And being alone and a long way from home is lots scarier than a mountaintop full of bears. Which is my crazy way of telling you how glad I am I found you...'cause being here with somebody important like you...it makes me think my dreams are coming true...*even if we are lost.*

HOWARD. We are *not* lost!

TAMMY. Then why are we here?

HOWARD. *(finally focusing on* **TAMMY***)* Poor baby's shaking.

TAMMY. I'm freezing, Howard!

HOWARD. I can fix that.

TAMMY. Fix it in the car, okay?

*(***TAMMY*** stands, attempts to step away from* **HOWARD***; he takes her hand)*

Howard...!

*(***HOWARD*** pulls* **TAMMY*** back to him; they kiss, long and passionately, at least he does.)*

HOWARD. *Now*...what do you think about the place?

TAMMY. It's still cold! I'm sorry, but it is. Plus – if we aren't lost – why *are* we here?

HOWARD. The stars! The view out there – !

TAMMY. Howard! You can't see anything out there! *It's dark!*

HOWARD. Well, it won't be dark Saturday.

TAMMY. We gotta come back? *(not pleased)*

HOWARD. Of course, were coming back, Annie!

TAMMY. Tammy. *(under her breath, leaving no doubt she's had to correct him before)*

HOWARD. It's what I've been searching for.

TAMMY. It's just an empty old store.

HOWARD. Who cares about the store? The land – the top of this mountain – that's what I want. And by Monday, it'll be mine.

TAMMY. *(something clicks, excitedly)* HOWARD! *Maybe are you talking about what I think maybe you're talking about?*

HOWARD. *Shhh...*

TAMMY. *This...*right here...*this is where you wanna make – ?*

HOWARD. I warned you, Tammy!

TAMMY. I wasn't gonna say it. *(obediently puts her hand over her mouth)*

HOWARD. Don't even think it.

TAMMY. I won't even think it. I promise.

HOWARD. 'Cause if anybody finds out –

TAMMY. They won't find out from me.

HOWARD. Anybody finds out...none of it will happen. All your dreams...gone.

TAMMY. Why is that, Howard? I don't understand.

HOWARD. Because it's our secret.

TAMMY. Okay ...

HOWARD. Because if somebody finds out what I'm up to –

TAMMY. Or that you're a really big-time... *(once again places her hands over her mouth)* Sorr...eee.

HOWARD. Somebody'll beat me to the punch.

TAMMY. They'll do what you're planning to do, huh?

HOWARD. Exactly.

TAMMY. And they won't include me.

HOWARD. They won't include you, Tammy.

TAMMY. Oh, I know, Howard. Sometimes I make up stories. Say the crazy things that keep popping into my head. But I'm not gonna tell anybody anything about what you're planning. And that means…! *(excitedly, perhaps clapping, twilling in circles to show her joy)* Oh, my God, Howard! That means…I'm gonna be the new…! *(puts her forefinger to her lips, knows not to say what she thinks she's going to be)* Shhhh, Tammy… *(takes* **HOWARD***'s hand in hers, looks into his eyes as if he were a god)* To think, Howard…yesterday I was a second-shift waitress with a silly dream…working my tail off in a dinky little diner…going nowhere except to the kitchen for pie and cake and change for a dollar. *Now –* thanks to you *– I'm gonna be the new… (once again successfully resists telling their secret)* Oh, Howard! You've changed my life! You've made me the happiest girl in the whole wide world! Thank you!

*(***TAMMY*** gives* **HOWARD** *a kiss he'll remember, then looks out over the mountains she can't see.)*

And it *is* beautiful up here. And perfect! Just like you said.

HOWARD. That's my baby.

(With the help of his flashlight, he returns to the aisle. After a moment, speaking to himself.)

Over here, I'll put the… *(doesn't finish his sentence, enthusiastically)* And over here…ah, yes, over here…!

*(***TAMMY*** watches* **HOWARD** *disappear into the dark. After a moment, she looks out, pauses. Then, in dramatic fashion – confident* **HOWARD** *won't hear – speaks as if Old Smokey were Tara and she were Scarlett O'Hara… only one far less talented than Vivian Leigh.)*

TAMMY. As God is my witness… *(clears her throat, more dramatic now)* As God is my witness, they're not going to lick me. I'm going to live through this and when it's over…I'll never go hungry again! *(with added determination, as if she were speaking for herself)* I'll never, *ever* go hungry again!

*(***TAMMY***, proud of herself and excited about her future, looks at the stars, smiles approvingly, then sings – softly at first – the spiritual "This Little Light of Mine.")*

"THIS LITTLE LIGHT OF MINE"

TAMMY.
> THIS LITTLE LIGHT OF MINE,
> I'M GONNA LET IT SHINE.
> THIS LITTLE LIGHT OF MINE,
> I'M GONNA LET IT SHINE.

> *(Motivated by a feeling of triumph,* **TAMMY** *begins to shuffle her feet to the music – perhaps using her flashlight as a spotlight – while singing with gusto.)*

> THIS LITTLE LIGHT OF MINE,
> I'M GONNA LET IT SHINE.
> LET IT SHINE,
> LET IT SHINE,
> LET IT SHINE!

> *(As* **TAMMY** *continues to dance and sing, lights dim to black and the music turns into a recording of the song. We hear it during the scene change.)*

End of Scene

Scene Three

(Next day, late afternoon, a Friday. **EMMA, JINKS** *and* **OLIVE** *have made minor progress in their clean-up effort. Still, Old Smokey is weeks away from re-opening, if only because the shelves remain empty of merchandise. A bowl of dip and a plate of crackers as well as a shopping bag now rest on the counter. Also, a guitar is now positioned against the counter.)*

*(**AT RISE** – as the spiritual heard during the scene change is down and out –* **JINKS** *parades around the space, detailing [if only to annoy* **OLIVE***] her ideas for the store's future. As she does,* **OLIVE** *observes; her expressions suggest she's biting her tongue to keep from jumping all over* **JINKS***.* **EMMA** *lets them carry on; her body language, however, makes it clear their bickering continues to disappoint her.)*

JINKS. Over here…shelves brim with soaps, syrups, fancy things from places we haven't even heard of. Next to them…exotic jellies, jams, relishes…*organic*, of course. *(crosses to the counter, dips a cracker into the bowl)* Including my very special…just for Olive…deep-south hummus.

*(**JINKS** takes a bite, then offers* **OLIVE** *a sample; she turns away.)*

OLIVE. Deep south…like hell!

*(**EMMA** crosses to the hummus, dips a cracker, takes a bite, seems to approve.* **OLIVE** *observes.)*

JINKS. Out there… *(points to the porch)* …where the view is something to write home about…travelers gather around wrought-iron tables, dining on delicate little sandwiches garnished with condiments from half a world away. Every delectable nibble catered by the talented chefs at Jinks' renowned "Gourmet Kitchen in the *Sticks*." And sweet tea? Forget it…bring on the jasmine.

OLIVE. Oh, Lord, Emma…she'll do to Old Smokey what's she's about to do to her "Fried-Free Zone."

EMMA. *(to* **JINKS**, *after taking another bite of the dip, impressed)* What am I tasting?

*(***OLIVE** *eases to the hummus, taking care that neither* **JINKS** *or* **EMMA** *see her.)*

JINKS. Well, I start with black-eyed peas…

(As **JINKS** *speaks,* **OLIVE** *bravely dips a cracker in the dish. She likes black-eyed peas.)*

Add a little garlic, some olive oil. And to give it that magically smooth taste…

*(***OLIVE** *takes a bite. What she doesn't know is* **JINKS** *sees her thus causing her to "customize" her list of ingredients.)*

Tofu mixed with anchovies.

(Upon hearing the nasty words "tofu" and "anchovies," **OLIVE** *spews the dip from her mouth.* **EMMA** *hands her a paper towel.)*

JINKS. *(grinning smugly, enjoying her latest "victory")* And over there…in an expansive new annex…our clothing and shoe departments –

OLIVE. *(cynically, laughing as she cleans up her mess)* Shoe department…

JINKS. Customers are gonna need boots to hike to our fabulous mountain-top theme park, appropriately called…"The Thrill on the Hill." Which is Phase Four of our twenty-five year expansion program.

OLIVE. Would you listen, Emma?

JINKS. And to fill up our brand-spanking new multi-story parking garages – I picture three, how many do you see, Olive? – we'll paint colorful signs on barns from Charlotte to Memphis urging folks to…*"See Old Smokey."* Of course, by then they'll be "Old Smokeys" everywhere thanks to our in-house franchising department.

(OLIVE *laughs, which further annoys* JINKS. EMMA *looks at both of the women, shakes her head disapprovingly.*)

JINKS Or maybe we'll just let Teddy sit on his butt, watch business go somewhere else because somebody doesn't have the imagination of a –

(*Before* JINKS *can say whatever it was she was about to say,* CORDELIA *– an attractive, talented, ambitious, excited young lady – explodes into Old Smokey.*)

CORDELIA. Guess what I just found out! *Teddy'll be home a week from today!*

EMMA. What?

CORDELIA. He just called, Miz Darlington! *(steps to* EMMA, *gives her a hug)*

OLIVE. They're sending him home early, Emma.

CORDELIA. That's good news. Don't you think?

JINKS. Of course, it's good news.

EMMA. It's wonderful news… *(looks at the work to be done, all but panicked)* Except Old Smokey…oh, Lord, it's no where close to being ready. I promised him, and it's… look at it…it's –

OLIVE. Hey, we'll get it done.

JINKS. After which, I'll cook him a welcome-home feast he won't forget. No tofu…no anchovies…and – if God isn't watching – *fried* with love.

(OLIVE *and* JINKS *give an anxious* EMMA *a hug, perhaps expressing their commitment to the task at hand. After which, the women spring into motion, undertaking various project [moving boxes, straightening signs, etc.] with renewed urgency. They converse as they work.*)

CORDELIA. I should've been helping yesterday. But I was… well, I was working.

OLIVE. We heard you on the radio.

EMMA. I didn't know you had a new job.

CORDELIA. It happened so quickly, Miz Darlington.

OLIVE. The station called Cordelia. Isn't that true, sweetie?

CORDELIA. After I sent them a CD. Of course, it's nothing permanent.

OLIVE. She's got her eyes set on Knoxville TV.

CORDELIA. That's not true, Mama. And I wish you'd quit saying it. *(to* **EMMA** *and* **JINKS** *as she works)* Mama thinks just because I like to pretend I'm doing the weather I want to be on TV next.

OLIVE. Show 'em, sweetie.

CORDELIA. Mama. Most TV weather folks are meteorologists. You have to go to college for that.

OLIVE. Go to college? To get the forecast wrong? *(in an announcer-like voice)* Ladies and gentlemen…here she is…your dazzling new Channel Eight weather-girl…the lovely watermelon queen herself…Cordelia Dunwitty…with your never-wrong, always-right, just-in-time…weather report.

CORDELIA. Mama. I don't want to do the weather!

OLIVE. She is so good. *Show 'em for me, Cordelia…!*

CORDELIA. *(giving in, doing the report in a sweet, almost professional manner)* If y'all looked outside you know things are looking good…sunny skies, temperature in the sixties. But watch out…'cause overnight skies will be turning cloudy…colder temperatures and maybe even some wind and storms…are heading our way. *(looks at* **OLIVE**, *smiles)* That's the weather, Mama.

OLIVE. Give us the forecast.

CORDELIA. I just did!

OLIVE. Use this as a pointer. *(hands a broom to* **CORDELIA***)*

CORDELIA. TV weather people don't use pointers anymore.

OLIVE. *Use the damn pointer, Cordelia!*

CORDELIA. Mama, you're driving me crazy! *(defiantly accepts the broom, points the handle in an upward direction; her anger builds as she goes along)* A late-season cold front is coming in from…somewhere way up here…it's headed straight down here… *(lowers the handle, continuing to point to an imaginary map)* Which is where we are…*smack-dab right here!* Trailing along up here… *(raises the bloom handle again)* …are storms, heavy rain, tornadoes, who knows what the hell else? Which by tomorrow could blow things – *including Old Smokey* – into the next county and beyond…causing holy hell and damnation everywhere in this *unfortunate bull's-eye right here…* *(moves the broom handle in a circle, increasingly unhappy about this forced show and tell)* …which is us! Now, Mama…I hope you're happy!

OLIVE. Isn't she a natural?

CORDELIA. You're embarrassing me, Mama.

OLIVE. Of course, nobody should be surprised, considering her mama was almost the Julia Child of her generation.

CORDELIA. Mama exaggerates sometimes.

OLIVE. Exaggerates, hell. Radio, TV…cookbooks –

JINKS. *(interrupting, in an official sounding voice)* Attention shoppers…now available in our book department… "Mastering The Art of…*Deep Frying*"

OLIVE. *(for once, successfully ignoring JINKS)* Paris, Rome, New York. Oh, I had it all planned out.

EMMA. Till something happened.

OLIVE. Till I came to my senses. Realized life was better here…where the grass is green, the mountains soar to the sky, where –

JINKS. What happened is…she married Jimmy Dunwitty.

OLIVE. *At least I got married…!*

JINKS. To an… *(mouthing the words, making sure CORDELIA doesn't see or hear her)* …un-der-tak-er.

OLIVE. *And who do you go home to?* Oh, I know…one of the many men you're dating who no one ever sees. Mystery men…all of them! I wonder why that is?

EMMA. *Can't anybody ever say anything nice?*

JINKS. *(after a moment, sweetly, perhaps taking* **CORDELIA***'s hand)* Cordelia, sugar…I thought your little presentation was…real good.

OLIVE. Well…*that* is truly an unexpected compliment.

JINKS. With your pretty voice, have you thought about doing things like…singing commercials?

OLIVE. She made one up for Jimmy's funeral business. Didn't you, sweetie?

CORDELIA. It was a joke. Daddy isn't going to let me use it.

OLIVE. Sing it, Cordelia!

CORDELIA. Mama! Why do you keep doing this to me?

OLIVE. Cordelia! We are waiting…!

(Somewhat reluctantly, at least at first, **CORDELIA** *sings the following to the tune "Over There." Try as she might, she can't keep from moving her legs and body to the beat, perhaps because deep down she's proud of her little ditty and has a good singing voice to boot.)*

"WAY UP THERE"

CORDELIA.
WAY UP THERE, OR WAY DOWN THERE,
SEND THE WORD, WE'LL SEND THE WORD, WAY UP THERE,
THAT YOU ARE COMING FROM DUNWITTY'S PLACE.
YOU'RE ALL DRESSED UP AND WE FIXED YOUR FACE.

SO PREPARE, WE'LL SAY A PRAYER,
WE'LL SEND THE WORD, SEND THE WORD, DO YOUR HAIR.
YOU'RE ON YOUR WAY, FOR YOUR NEW DAY,
AND WE WON'T LEAVE YOU, TILL IT'S OVER, WAY UP THERE!

*(***CORDELIA** *gives a crisp military salute, as* **JINKS** *and* **OLIVE** *applaud enthusiastically, that is until they realize they're agreeing on something.)*

OLIVE. Now sing that other little song you've been playing with.

*(An exasperated **CORDELIA** stares at **OLIVE**, then picks up the guitar, strums it for a moment and then – still starring at her mama – obediently sings the following to the tune of "Hard Rock Candy Mountain." She isn't pleased and it shows.)*

"OLD SMOKEY COUNTRY STORE"

CORDELIA.
OH, THE PLAYING OF THE FIDDLE AND THE TELLING OF A RIDDLE
AT A PLACE YOU CAN'T IGNORE
BY THE LEMONADE STAND WHERE THE VIEW IS GRAND
OLD SMOKEY COUNTRY STORE.

ONE MORNING AS THE SUN CAME UP
AND THE EARLY DEW WAS LIFTING
UP THE ROAD CAME A MAN A-HIKING.
HE SAID, "FOLKS, I'M NOT DRIFTING."
I'M HEADED FOR A PLACE THAT'S UP THE ROAD
AND FILLED WITH SO MUCH MORE.
SO COME WITH ME AND WE'LL GO SEE
OLD SMOKEY COUNTRY STORE.

*(**OLIVE** rushes to **CORDELIA**'s side and together they repeat the refrain.)*

CORDELIA & OLIVE.
OH, THE PLAYING OF THE FIDDLE AND THE TELLING OF A RIDDLE
AT A PLACE YOU CAN'T IGNORE
BY THE LEMONADE STAND WHERE THE VIEW IS GRAND
OLD SMOKEY COUNTRY STORE!

*(As **EMMA** and **JINKS** applaud, **CORDELIA** hands the guitar to **OLIVE**.)*

CORDELIA. Now, Mama…sing one of your songs. The one you keep telling me was the "hit" you and Miz Wilkins had when *you were civil to one another.*

OLIVE. I've forgotten the words.

CORDELIA. You sing it to yourself everyday.

EMMA. I'd love to hear the two of you sing together one more time.

OLIVE. I assure you none of us will live that long! *(sets the guitar down)*

JINKS. *Amen!* Which brings us back to commercials. Whatdaya got for restaurants?

OLIVE. *Oh, no you don't!*

JINKS. Something toe-tapping like... *(sings the opening of* **CORDELIA***'s proposed commercial)*
...WAY UP THERE, OR WAY DOWN THERE...

CORDELIA. I'll come up with something, Miz Wilkins –

OLIVE. *(to* **CORDELIA***, becoming increasingly emotional)* Over my dead body will anybody in my family endorse her Yankee-loving so-called restaurant to-be! Anymore than her *fricking* bookstore –

CORDELIA. Mama!

OLIVE. Which she ran into the ground! Books on organic gardening. On that so-called global warming nonsense. Shelves of high-brow English literature, of all the boring crap –

EMMA. Olive! This isn't helping!

OLIVE. Not a single sizzling *Southern* romance in the lot! *So forget it, Cordelia!*

(A disgusted **EMMA** *has heard enough. She steps out to the porch.)*

CORDELIA. This is business, Mama!

OLIVE. *Well, I never...!*

JINKS. With that lovely show of emotion, I'm off. *(steps to exit, looking at* **OLIVE***)* But I will return...before things start falling *from the heavens.*

*(***OLIVE** *follows* **JINKS***, now angrier than ever.)*

OLIVE. *From the heavens?*

CORDELIA. Mama, don't you see what Miz Wilkins keeps doing – ?

(**JINKS**, *pleased she's really gotten to* **OLIVE**, *exits to the porch. An increasingly angry* **OLIVE** *ignores* **CORDELIA**, *follows.*)

OLIVE. *FROM THE NORTH!* Freezing temperatures, ice, snow…who knows what the hell else?…ruining another perfectly lovely *Southern* spring day.

CORDELIA. She keeps egging you on.

OLIVE. *(to* **EMMA***)* Wanna know why *she* despises everything Southern? Because folks down here don't cater to her…*liberal* ideas!

JINKS. *(proudly, to* **CORDELIA***)* Oh, I *do* know how to ring her bell.

OLIVE. Of course, when she went up *there*… *(points "north")* Oh, she was gonna make her fortune! Till she found out she was too liberal even for those *damn Yankees*. So, she tucked her tail and scurried home…like an old hound dog.

JINKS. 'Cause I missed *you*, Olive.

OLIVE. *(also to* **EMMA***)* And our singing act! Wanna know why it broke up?

EMMA. No. But you'll tell me anyway.

OLIVE. Because *she* wanted us to sing songs that serve the Devil!

JINKS. Songs about drinking and cheating, right?

OLIVE. And *sexual…affairs!*

CORDELIA.	**EMMA.**
Oh, Mama…	Olive!

OLIVE. While I insisted on singing hymns, gospels…songs my mama taught me. Like Ruth in the Scriptures, *I* remained loyal to God.

JINKS. So you're Ruth...*with a potty mouth.* And I'm...*who...?*

OLIVE. Well, I don't know for sure. But the name *Jezebel* keeps coming to mind.

JINKS. *(remembers something else she expects will "ring* **OLIVE***'s bell")* With all the huffing and puffing, I almost forgot... *(crosses to the counter, picks up a shopping bag, removes three aprons, returns to* **CORDELIA** *and* **EMMA***, presents one to each)* Go on...try them on...one size fits all.

*(***EMMA** *and* **CORDELIA** *tie on the aprons, then model them. They read "Old Smokey." We sense* **OLIVE** *feels a bit left out.)*

EMMA.	**CORDELIA.**
Thank you.	How nice, Miz Wilkins.

JINKS. Oh, I've got something for you too, Olive...to celebrate your unique standing in our little community. *(hands a third apron to* **OLIVE***)*

*(***OLIVE** *– more than a wee bit leery – accepts the apron, takes a look at it. Expressionless, she slips it on, models it for the others who expect her to explode because – in big, bold letters – it reads, "QUEEN OF THE SOUTH.")*

CORDELIA. It looks nice on you, Mama.

OLIVE. *(after a moment, smiling broadly, dripping with sweetness)* How ever do I thank you, Jinks?

CORDELIA. I'm proud of you, Mama.

*(***JINKS***, caught off guard, doesn't know how to respond. Thus, she picks up her bucket, mop, looks back at* **OLIVE** *who continues to appear pleased, exits in a huff. Score one for* **OLIVE***.)*

OLIVE. While some folks *disappear.* Others have work to do...including the store room and office, such as it is... *(straightens her apron, then opens the door to the side office, horrified at the sight)* Oh, Lord!

(Bravely, **OLIVE** *exits into the adjoining room, closing the door after her. As she does,* **CORDELIA** *joins* **EMMA** *on the porch.)*

EMMA. They are two big pains in the butt...

(**EMMA** *and* **CORDELIA** *smile at one another, then work in silence until* **CORDELIA** *stops, looks out.*)

CORDELIA. What a view, huh? The sun fixing to set over those mountains...

EMMA. At night – dark as it gets up here – the stars take your breath away.

CORDELIA. I probably shouldn't say this, but that's when Teddy... *(excitedly)* Can you believe it, Miz Darlington? He'll be here in a week! That's when we'd drive up here. Sit in his old truck. In fact, that's where he proposed...right out there. We'd talk for hours, listen to the radio. Did you know...up here, you can hear stations from just about everywhere? Then, we'd... *(stops short of saying something she shouldn't)* Then we'd look at the stars some more...till it was time to go home. Which was always way too late as far as mama was concerned. *(pause)* Teddy said your daddy would come out here most Saturday nights, play his fiddle. He said folks would drive up from everywhere.

EMMA. Out of the hills for sure.

CORDELIA. So many...the parking lot would fill up. Is that true?

EMMA. Get here early or you wouldn't find a spot.

CORDELIA. And when it got dark, drivers would shine their headlights on the porch?

EMMA. They'd light it up...like spotlights in a fancy theatre. After which they'd fill the porch...carry on – singing, playing –

CORDELIA. Including you. Isn't that true?

EMMA. The boy we love can't keep his mouth shut. *(smiles, then after a moment, takes a deep breath, tells her story)* When the daddy you love expects you to be a part of something important like a Saturday night music show you don't disappoint.

CORDELIA. So...

EMMA. *So* I picked a song and practiced and practiced. Stood in front of a mirror a hundred times till I could tell myself, "I have heard worse." Then one night – as the lot filled and the stars came out – I gathered my courage, stood about here, and...would you believe?... began to sing. Until I discovered I wasn't looking into my mirror any more. In front of me were a hundred cars, their lights shining like I was on the stage of the Grand Ole Opry. At which point I froze, ran down the steps, disappeared behind the biggest tree I could find. I had had my fill of show business.

CORDELIA. Of course, you're sort of still in it –

EMMA. My beauty shop, huh?

(**CORDELIA** *puts the broom down, picks up the guitar, sits on a step, from time to time picks out a note or two as she listens to* **EMMA.**)

There I stood. Tears rolling down my cheek, thinking my life had ended. Which is when a handsome boy – who I'd never laid eyes on – appeared. He handed me his bandana – which, frankly, his mama should've washed...told me his name was Ben –

CORDELIA. Teddy's daddy! So what started out as a nightmare –

EMMA. Turned out to be the best night of my life.

CORDELIA. I love that story, Miz Darlington.

EMMA. As I was saying...before you got me telling tales on myself...folks would carry on up here till the wee hours of the morning

CORDELIA. It does sound like the Grand Old Opry.

EMMA. What it was...was "Saturday Night at Old Smokey." *(reminiscing fondly)* Standing here...on a beautiful September night eons ago...your mama and Jinks sang together for the first time. "Amazing Grace!" It never sounded so pretty.

CORDELIA. Gosh, I'd love to have heard them.

EMMA. Peek into my office...see what's left...fiddles, more guitars, tambourines, an old washboard.

(**CORDELIA** *now picks out the opening notes of the song "Cumberland Gap" which* **EMMA** *knows. She sings the first few words.*)

"CUMBERLAND GAP"

EMMA.
LAY DOWN, BOYS, AND TAKE A LITTLE NAP...

(**EMMA** *hesitates, which causes* **CORDELIA** *to complete the opening line of the song.*)

CORDELIA.
WE'RE ALL GOING DOWN TO CUMBERLAND GAP.

CORDELIA & EMMA.
CUMBERLAND GAP, CUMBERLAND GAP,
WE'RE ALL GOING DOWN TO CUMBERLAND GAP...

EMMA.
SAVE UP SOME MONEY AND BUY ME A FARM
RAISE SOME 'TATERS AS LONG AS YOUR ARM.
AS LONG AS YOUR ARM, LONG AS YOUR ARM,
RAISE SOME 'TATERS AS LONG AS YOUR ARM.

CORDELIA.
TEDDY'S COMING HOME TO CUMBERLAND GAP,
WE'LL ALL BE HOME AT CUMBERLAND GAP.

CORDELIA & EMMA.
CUMBERLAND GAP, CUMBERLAND GAP,
WE'LL ALL BE HOME AT CUMBERLAND GAP.

CORDELIA. Who needs the Mountain Mamas, huh?

EMMA. Since we're singing about Teddy. He knows about your job?

CORDELIA. It's not really a job-job. But I've talked to him, sure. I also told him someday I'd like to do real reporting...like they do at the networks...from "remote locations." Which is when I remembered something big is happening here. Old Smokey's reopening. Teddy's almost home. So I'm thinking I'd like to interview you.. We could talk about the night Teddy said somebody real famous ended up here –

EMMA. *That* was another night to remember!

CORDELIA. And I'd like to do it tomorrow afternoon. A special…"Cordelia In The PM…*Live from Old Smokey.*" Is that really dumb?

*(Silence as **EMMA** considers the idea.)*

The station loved the idea. I'll bring everything we need. We can practice first.

EMMA. *(after a moment, smiling)* I believe it…sounds like fun.

CORDELIA. Oh, thank you!

*(Again the women work in silence. After a moment, **EMMA** bravely speaks what's really on her mind.)*

EMMA. He'll look the same, of course.

CORDELIA. That's the part I'm really looking forward to.

EMMA. But the injury…the… *(The words are hard for her to say.)*

CORDELIA. Traumatic brain injury. TBI for short. I looked it all up on the internet.

EMMA. You know what to expect.

CORDELIA. I know what an improvised explosive device can do to somebody…yes, Ma'am.

EMMA. He'll be confused. Is that right?

CORDELIA. It's possible…

EMMA. Anxious. Maybe a little depressed. Not able to remember things like he used to.

CORDELIA. If you're asking if he'll struggle some…yes, Ma'am. I think so.

EMMA. Then tell me I'm right. Running this place – with a little help from me, maybe you – it'll give him a chance to heal in a place he loves. Help him get his feet back on the ground –

CORDELIA. Help him be the Teddy we remember.

EMMA. That's all true. Isn't it?

CORDELIA. Lord, I hope so, Miz Darlington. *(realizes her words aren't as comforting as* **EMMA** *needs)* What are you saying, Cordelia? When Teddy gets home next week… steps out here…looks at his mountains…breaths this fresh mountain air…in no time at all…it'll be like he never left. *(looks at* **EMMA**, *softly, reassuringly)* Promise.

*(***CORDELIA*** smiles at ***EMMA***, who manages to return the smile. Both are hopeful, but we understand neither is certain their shared wish will become reality. After a moment,* **EMMA** *moves her hands across her body, taking hold of her opposite forearm, as if she were chilled. As the women look out over their treasured mountains – and as lights slowly fade to black – we hear the hymn "Amazing Grace!" It is sung by a female duet…could it be we're hearing* **JINKS** *and* **OLIVE***'s first performance at Old Smokey? The hymn continues through the scene change.)*

End of Scene

Scene Four

(Late afternoon, the following day, a Saturday. **JINKS'** *dip has been removed and – in general – things appear more orderly.)*

(AT RISE – as the hymn comes down – we see only **JINKS** *who's in the process of removing items of merchandise [perhaps jars or boxes] from a larger box. As she places items on shelves, she looks at the audience. For a moment, those sitting out front may believe she's talking to them.)*

JINKS. I was born in Alabama…when my daddy was in the army. I think you know that. But what I never told anybody – including *you* – *was our dirty little secret…*

*(***JINKS** *– still looking out – waits patiently, knowing* **EMMA** *will eventually open the door to the office/store room to hear her "secret." After a long moment – unable to resist –* **EMMA** *emerges.)*

EMMA. *All right! Tell me!*

JINKS. They got me mixed up in the hospital.

EMMA. You can do better than that.

JINKS. *It's true – !*

EMMA. Yeah, right. *(disappointed, she reenters the office/store room)*

JINKS. *(speaking loudly so as to be heard in the adjoining room)* Instead of going home with that nice family I belonged to…to Wisconsin or Minnesota…some place you can go outside in summer without melting…I ended up here …

(Once again, **EMMA** *emerges from the store room; this time she struggles with a box.* **JINKS** *gives her a hand.)*

EMMA. While some unknown, unsuspecting, *fortunate* woman ended up in Milwaukee or Minneapolis –

JINKS. Chicago – who knows?

EMMA. She should be here –

JINKS. I should be up there! Explains a lot, doesn't it…?

EMMA. Why you're so dead-set against everything Southern …from fried chicken –

JINKS. To okra, catfish –

EMMA. Cornbread, Southern accents –

JINKS. *Humidity* –

EMMA. You can't help it.

JINKS. *No way! I'm a Yankee!* And to our very own Queen of the South –

EMMA. *That's* a dirty little secret.

JINKS. However, being a resourceful Yankee-wannabe…I'm making cranberry juice out of cranberries. I'm writing a tell-all destined for every bookshelf north of Louisville… *"An Unclaimed Yankee…Lost In The Heart Of Dixie."*

EMMA. If you share that with the "Queen," make sure it's somewhere I'm not. Now I've got business to tend to. *(smiles, takes* **JINKS**' *hand in hers)* Yankee or not…I don't know what I'd do without you.

*(***EMMA*** exits into the store room/office. As she does,* **JINKS** *starts removing items from* **EMMA***'s box. After a moment,* **CORDELIA** *enters. She wears a jacket – the colder weather she'd forecast has arrived – and carries equipment of the type a radio station might use to broadcast from a remote location [see Property List for a suggestion], including a microphone [perhaps bearing the WRET call letters]. She places the equipment on the counter.)*

CORDELIA. Mornin', Miz Wilkins.

JINKS. Morning to you, Cordelia.

(Sees the equipment, nods in that direction, which **CORDELIA** *notes)*

CORDELIA. In the radio business, you never know when you'll find a good story.

JINKS. Oh, I know all about your broadcast this afternoon. Emma told me.

CORDELIA. She *is* here?

JINKS. In there...

CORDELIA. Mornin', Miz Darlington.

EMMA. *(offstage)* Mornin', Cordelia.

*(**CORDELIA** begins setting up her equipment. As she works, we hear the sound of wind outside Old Smokey.)*

JINKS. Listen to that wind. Of course, it isn't like we didn't know something ugly was coming our way.

CORDELIA. Even weather people get lucky once in a while.

*(As **CORDELIA** sets up the equipment, she hums the first few lines of the song "On Top of Old Smokey." **JINKS** can't resist singing the song as she knows it.)*

JINKS.
ON TOP OF OLD SMOKEY,
ALL COVERED WITH SNOW...

*(**CORDELIA** joins in and they sing the next line in unison.)*

CORDELIA & JINKS.
I LOST MY TRUE LOVER,
FOR COURTIN' TOO SLOW.

JINKS. If ever there were a song for this old place...

CORDELIA. That's what I was thinking! So I worked it into a little commercial ...

*(A confident, enthusiastic **CORDELIA** begins to sing "On Top Of Old Smokey," into the microphone, only this time substituting her words.)*

"OUR NAME IS OLD SMOKEY"

CORDELIA.
OUR NAME IS OLD SMOKEY,
WE'RE A GREAT STORE.
ONCE YOU HAVE BEEN HERE,
YOU'LL COME BACK FOR MORE

JINKS. Would you listen to that...?

CORDELIA.
>WE'LL FILL YOU WITH FOOD,
>AND SELL YOU OUR STUFF.
>OUR SPOT IS SO PRETTY,
>YOU'LL FIND LEAVING IS TOUGH.
>
>*(Now reading from a sheet of paper in her best radio voice)*
>
>Once upon a time, there was a very special store at the top of the most beautiful mountain anywhere. News spread and folks came from "Miles Around" and "Hither and Yon" to marvel at the view and pick up goodies they couldn't find anywhere else. Well, the good news is Old Smokey Country Store is still around. The really great news is, it's fixin' to reopen...offering a shopping adventure you won't find anywhere else. So come up and visit, especially if you're from *"Miles Around"* or *"Hither and Yon"* or even... *"Somewhere-in-Between."* Discover why we're so special...somebody even wrote a song about us... *(sings again, this time with added gusto)*
>
>SO PLEASE COME TO SEE US,
>THERE'S NOTHING TO FEAR.
>WE'LL TREAT YOU LIKE FAMILY,
>SO, COME UP, YOU HEAR?
>
>That's Old Smokey Country Store...top of the mountain...just south of town.

JINKS. *(applauding enthusiastically)* Now all we need is something for my restaurant. I'm dying to hear your ideas.

CORDELIA. I'll give you good ones. And I won't charge anything.

JINKS. You *will* be paid...considering your mama's gonna kill you.

CORDELIA. Mama's all talk. She doesn't even own a gun.

JINKS. She'll do you in with words, including some four-letter doozies. And frankly, my dear, I'd prefer a double-barrel shotgun.

(**JINKS** *smiles as* **CORDELIA** *puts the finishing touches to her equipment set up.*)

Before y'all become big-time radio stars, may I ask something that's none of my business?

CORDELIA. Sure…

JINKS. How will you juggle everything? Teddy coming home sooner than we thought…helping some here…your new career?

CORDELIA. Everybody keeps saying working at the radio station's a new career. It's not. Because it's not what I want to do. And don't ask me what that is…I have no idea. All I know is before Teddy left we talked about lots of things, but mostly about Old Smokey –

JINKS. It's been a big part of his life –

CORDELIA. From the moment he started refilling candy jars for his granddaddy –

JINKS. To when he and his daddy would work up here all day, then sit on the porch, watch the sun go down –

CORDELIA. Talk till they couldn't hear each other over the crickets. He's shared everything with me, Miz Wilkins. Including plans I probably shouldn't talk about.

JINKS. I understand –

CORDELIA. *(she's not about to keep the secret, excitedly)* He wants to turn Old Smokey from a country store into a kind of an outdoor adventure store! He'd sell…we'd sell…fishing and hunting equipment – everything but guns, I told him I don't like guns, and I don't think he does anymore…plus camping stuff, outdoor gear. In time we'd do the things you'd do…have a catalog, be on the internet –

JINKS. A warning, Cordelia....have nothing to do with something that needs a password to google, browse and *crash*.

CORDELIA. I'm just saying you have wonderful ideas. Your book store. Before that, the ladies' dress shop. Now your restaurant.

JINKS. And never take advice from somebody whose business motto is "I can only fail and embarrass myself so many times." What's important is...*I love the store idea!*

CORDELIA. Teddy thinks – and I do too – we can make it a destination store...kind of like once-upon-a-time Old Smokey was a destination for people who wanted to sing and play music on Saturday nights. Of course, with everything that's happened...we'll have to be patient. But my fingers are crossed...he gets home... good things'll happen...maybe even faster than his doctors imagined. At least that's what I'm praying.

JINKS. *(sensing **CORDELIA**'s fear)* A little old injury isn't gonna keep Teddy from getting what he wants.

CORDELIA. It's not such a *little* old injury.

JINKS. Can I tell you something without you telling him?

*(**CORDELIA** nods.)*

That boy – bless his heart – doesn't have one iota of God-given football talent in his entire body.

CORDELIA. He was all-everything in high school.

JINKS. Because he was determined to run faster, throw the ball further. Oh, I know very little about business and even less about football, but I do know something about Teddy Darlington...he sets his mind on something, nothing'll slow him down. Nothing...okay?

*(We hear the opening notes of "Dixie" played on **OLIVE**'s air horn. **CORDELIA** rolls her eyes, causing **JINKS** to comment.)*

JINKS. Look at it this way, Cordelia. Some Southern women wear their hair long, teased high, sprayed tight and over dyed. Others dip their drawling voices to a purr every time a man's in the neighborhood. Your mama – bless her true Southern heart – simply toots the wrong horn at all the wrong times.

CORDELIA. You don't know half of it. And don't ask me what that is because she *will* kill me.

JINKS. My mouth is sealed.

CORDELIA. Last week she insisted on driving that ugly red truck in Walker Cobb's funeral procession.

JINKS. I'm imagining the possibilities.

CORDELIA. Everything was fine till they lifted Mr. Cobb out of Daddy's hearse. Which is when she must've hit something, causing the rebel flag on her truck to flash and dance like it was in Las Vegas and Elvis was still in the building.

JINKS. This is making my day!

CORDELIA. Which made her furious. So she started shouting words I didn't even think she knew. Most of which nobody heard, 'cause just about then... *(sings the words)* "*I Wish I Was In The Land of Cotton*" started roaring out of the horn. Daddy said it was so loud it could've waked up the dead...including poor Mr. Cobb.

JINKS. Who needs Gabriel when your mama's around?

CORDELIA. Daddy also said she can't go to any more funerals he's got anything to do with...unless it's her own.

(**OLIVE** *enters wearing a jacket and carrying a vase of flowers. As she does,* **JINKS** *smiles, then sings – in response to* **OLIVE**'s *"Dixie" – the opening words to "The Battle Hymn of the Republic."*)

JINKS.
MINE EYES HAVE SEEN THE GLORY
OF THE COMING OF THE LORD...

OLIVE. *(removing her jacket, proudly showing off her "Queen of the South" apron)* I'll have you know my mama's side of the family fought and died with Robert E. Lee!

CORDELIA. And your daddy's side sang, "Glory, glory, hallelujah!"

OLIVE. *Those people…we don't talk about!* *(places the flowers in a vase)* A little something to brighten things up.

JINKS. From your garden I bet.

(OLIVE ignores JINKS' question.)

Then you must've bought them, right?

(Again, OLIVE ignores JINKS' question.)

Well, if you didn't grow them. And you didn't buy them. You must've –

OLIVE. *(exploding) All right! They are funeral flowers!*

CORDELIA. Mama, you didn't –

OLIVE. Take them from the gravesite? *I did no such thing!* *(pointing toward the parking lot)* Who do you suppose those two are?

CORDELIA. *(also looking out)* Just kind of looking around.

OLIVE. *(continuing to look toward the parking lot)* Emma…

CORDELIA. In her office –

(OLIVE takes a step toward the office.)

JINKS. And doesn't want to be bothered.

OLIVE. I'll just work on my own…

(OLIVE picks up a cloth and begins dusting the various wall decorations. At the same time, JINKS resumes her chore, perhaps whistling the first few notes of the Battle Hymn of the Republic which, in turn, causes OLIVE to respond with a note or two of "Dixie." For a thirty seconds or so, the women work independently without speaking or acknowledging the other, still always knowing where the other is and not much caring for the idea she's anywhere

around. During their "dance of avoidance" we hear the RING of a telephone in **EMMA***'s office. About that time,* **JINKS** *has had enough of the play acting.)*

JINKS. Cordelia…I have something to tell your mama.

CORDELIA. *(fears* **JINKS** *will tell the funeral story)* Miz Wilkins…

JINKS. More important than that. I bet, Olive, you didn't know…I was born in Alabama.

OLIVE. How sad for Alabama.

JINKS. However, I grew up here.

OLIVE. Tennessee as well.

JINKS. What's important… *(picks up* **CORDELIA***'s mike, speaks into it.)* Are you listening, east Tennessee? They mixed me up in the hospital! *Which means,* if things had gone the way they should've, *I'd be up there…!* *(points up in a highly animated fashion)*

OLIVE. *(steps to the mike, speaks into it)* While I'm down *here…!* *(points down in an equally animated fashion)*

JINKS. We wouldn't have ever laid eyes on one another!

OLIVE. And what a wonderful world that would be!

CORDELIA. Mama, you don't mean that.

JINKS. And I assure everybody my first name wouldn't be Jinks. And I wouldn't be surrounded by rednecks addressing me – *when I am by myself* – as *"y'all."* Or, after asking a simple question, hearing, *"Do What Now?* Nor would I be fighting a losing war against people who have no idea how closed minded they are, how –

(A troubled – and now angry – **EMMA** *emerges from her office.* **JINKS** *and* **OLIVE***, sensing* **EMMA***'s concern, step away from the microphone. As they do, we hear a crack of distant thunder.)*

OLIVE. I hope you're listening, Emma. She's talking about you too.

EMMA. I'm doing more than listening. I'm about to forget the mess here. Fall on my knees, pray Teddy finds another way to get his feet on the ground. Go back to my beauty shop – God knows I've neglected it way too long – fix hair of women who can get along in public –

OLIVE. *(to* **JINKS***)* Look what you've done!

EMMA. Stop worrying about things…including now…how I'm going to pay taxes –

JINKS. They're overdue?

EMMA. They told me not to worry about them. Now they want the money Monday morning.

OLIVE. The day after tomorrow.

EMMA. If I don't have it…I'm not at the courthouse by nine a.m.… *(can't bring herself to completing her thought)*

JINKS. They wouldn't dare foreclose…

(Silence as the women look at one another)

OLIVE. Tell us how we can help.

EMMA. Start being civil. If *that's* possible I suppose anything is –

JINKS. Not only will we be civil –

OLIVE. We'll work together.

(After a second, **OLIVE** *and* **JINKS** *join hands. Neither likes the idea but they manage to smile at one another.)*

JINKS. It's a beginning, Emma.

EMMA. More like a miracle.

(A crack of thunder after which the store's lights blink off, then return. From this point to the end of the scene, the thunder grows louder.)

OLIVE. All I know is there's money in death, and Jimmy's checkbook is brimming with cash. How much do you need?

JINKS. No charity –

OLIVE. Pay it off when the store opens –

EMMA. With prayers and God's grace, we've kept these doors open for sixty years. I'd rather see them take it... tear it down, if that's what somebody's got in mind... then be beholden to anybody.

JINKS. We'll be creative... *(looks at* **OLIVE** *for help)*

OLIVE. Don't look at me...you're the one with the crazy ideas.

JINKS. Well...I suppose we could... *(for once, she's stumped)*

OLIVE. If it's Monday before you come up with something...forget it.

CORDELIA. I have an idea, Mrs. Darlington. But maybe you won't like it.

JINKS. She'll love it...we're desperate.

CORDELIA. Instead of the afternoon radio program we talked about –

EMMA. The interview program.

CORDELIA. Yes, Ma'am. Now, here's where it really does get crazy...this evening we'll do a "Saturday Night at Old Smokey" show...live...from out there. *(points to the porch)*

(We hear the sound of wind as well as another crack of thunder. Once again the lights blink off then back on.)

EMMA. We'd need singers and musicians...

CORDELIA. Introducing...the "Mountain Mamas." *(looks at* **OLIVE** *and* **JINKS***)*

OLIVE. Now, hold your horses, Cordelia.

CORDELIA. You said you said you wanted to help. We'll accept contributions –

EMMA. You know what I said about handouts –

CORDELIA. I'm not talking handouts, Miz Darlington. I'm talking about offering good old country entertainment...live and in person. Everybody'll want to be a part of it –

JINKS. Especially when they find out it's to save Old Smokey –

CORDELIA. And why saving it is so important.

EMMA. But tonight? How do you expect people to know?

CORDELIA. *(into the microphone)* "Ladies and Gentlemen… y'all join us this evening for a live "Saturday Night at Old Smokey" musical jamboree." The parking lot won't be big enough.

OLIVE. I'll do my part. I'll personally chauffer folks up here.

CORDELIA. Mama, I don't think anybody wants to ride in your truck.

OLIVE. Truck, hell. I'm borrowing your daddy's shiny new super-duper ten-passenger limousine. And if we find another driver, we'll load up the hearse! Let's just hope nobody died today.

(The lights blink on and off again. We hear more thunder.)

EMMA. What about the storm…?

CORDELIA. It'll pass.

(Another crack of thunder, this one louder than the first.)

Hey, who's the weathergirl?

JINKS. Emma…whatdaya think?

EMMA. I guess I think…what do we have to lose?

*(We hear another particularly loud crack of thunder as **CORDELIA** – concerned about the weather – crosses to the radio, turns it on. We hear the voice of an announcer.)*

ANNOUNCER. *(offstage)* I don't have to tell y'all we're experiencing strong wind and heavy rain throughout the W-R-E-T listening area. Now hold on…I've been handed a warning from the weather folks…this one's for y'all in –

(Lights in the store blink off, then back on, then off again. Suddenly Old Smokey has lost power, thus we no longer hear the announcer.)

EMMA. Oh, Lord…

*(Abruptly, **TAMMY** appears on the porch. She's hardly dressed for either the weather or a trip to the country.)*

TAMMY. Yo-hoo. Anybody here?

JINKS. Come in … before you're blown away…

TAMMY. *(enters, brushing rain from the shoulders of her very flashy outfit)* Our car slipped off the road. We were hoping somebody could pull us out.

EMMA. We'll do what we can –

TAMMY. I told him, of course. Before all this happened. I said, Howard, what are we doing up here again?

OLIVE. Why *are* you here?

TAMMY. I'm afraid I can't say. Well, I can say, but I shouldn't. What's important is…here we are. And we're stuck!

CORDELIA. *(she's been looking at the parking lot)* Not anymore…

TAMMY. *(looking out, waving to **HOWARD**)* Look what that remarkable man's been able to do…

EMMA. Your husband?

TAMMY. Why…I suppose he is.

(Abruptly the lights in the store return along with the radio. The storm, however, continues to rage.)

ANNOUNCER. *(offstage)* Again, folks in Johnson County are advised that storms…

CORDELIA. *(points toward the parking lot, excitedly)* The tree…I think it's gonna fall!

(All now look out.)

ANNOUNCER. *(offstage)* Heavy rain…

OLIVE. *It is falling…!*

ANNOUNCER. *(offstage)* And a tornado are approaching.
JINKS. *It's gonna hit the car!*
ANNOUNCER. *(offstage)* So, if you're in the area…
TAMMY. *IT'S COMING DOWN ON YOU, HOWARD…!*
ANNOUNCER. *(offstage) TAKE COVER!*
EMMA. *…AND DOWN ON OLD SMOKEY!*

*(The women duck, covering their heads with their hands. Moments later, we hear a loud ROAR followed by a CRASHING sound as if something has fallen on Old Smokey. At the same time, lights in the store [as well as the radio] flicker, then go out, casting the set in darkness and an eerie silence. After a moment – as a light-hearted suggestion of the "doom" seemingly facing **EMMA** and the others – we hear a spiritual, perhaps a sedate "Swing Low, Sweet Chariot.")*

End of Act One

ACT TWO

Scene One

(Old Smokey's sales area, moments following the end of Act I. Because electrical power remains out, several candles have been lit, giving the interior of the store [with the help of a few unseen stage lights] an intimate look. If we look carefully we can see a tree branch resting on the porch, obviously the result of the storm that ended Act I. An occasional flash of lightning and a loud clap of thunder tell us the storm remains in the area.)

*(At rise, **TAMMY**, **EMMA** and **JINKS** hover over **HOWARD** who is slumped in a chair and who – we'll soon discover – is being comforted after having been pulled from his car which was struck by the tree that also struck Old Smokey. At the same time, **OLIVE** looks out at the parking lot. There's a sense of urgency – perhaps even a bit of panic – in the air.)*

OLIVE. *(calling loudly to an unseen **CORDELIA** in the parking lot)* WHAT ARE THEY SAYING?

*(**EMMA** steps to the porch, looks out, sees the tree. **JINKS** joins her, takes her hand in hers. We sense they fear that their plans are in jeopardy.)*

I CAN'T HEAR YOU, CORDELIA.

TAMMY. Howard, please tell me you're gonna be okay.

*(**TAMMY** kneels at **HOWARD**'s side. He moans. As he does, **JINKS** and **EMMA** return to the others.)*

OLIVE. *(continuing to relay information)* THEY'RE SAYING WE'VE HAD A TORNADO.

JINKS. We don't need a car radio to tell us that.

OLIVE. THERE'S DAMAGE IN TOWN –

EMMA. Olive, we can hear you.

OLIVE. Trees down…roads closed –

CORDELIA. *(as she enters)* Including the only road up here.

EMMA. Oh, Lord!

TAMMY. Does that mean we're trapped?

(**EMMA**, **OLIVE**, **JINKS** *and* **CORDELIA** *look at one another;* **TAMMY** *takes that as a "yes" and is horrified.*)

We're trapped! And Howard! *He needs to go to the hospital!*

HOWARD. No…!

TAMMY. If he hadn't just moved the car. Howard, it fell right where you parked it.

HOWARD. I'm all right. *(managing to struggle to his feet)*

TAMMY. Tell him his car's a mess…so he *can't* be all right.

HOWARD. See? I'm doing…just…fine. *(attempts to take a step, feels faint, returns to the chair)*

TAMMY. Told you, Howard.

EMMA. Howard, my name is Emma. These ladies are Olive, Jinks and Cordelia. We want to help. What can we do?

TAMMY. Call nine-one-one!

EMMA. Cell phones don't work up here –

CORDELIA. And the regular phone lines are down, so –

TAMMY. *Oh, Howard…don't die on me!*

EMMA. I don't think he's going to die.

TAMMY. I hope not because he's… *(stops short of saying what she had planned to say)*

EMMA. He's your husband – we understand.

TAMMY. Plus he's…well he's a…*very* famous –

HOWARD. *Tammy!*

(**JINKS**, **OLIVE** and **CORDELIA** *look at* **TAMMY**, *expecting her to continue. She does, quite obvious saying whatever pops into her head.*)

TAMMY. Chef. A world renowned…gourmet chef. That's what he is.

JINKS. You're kidding me.

TAMMY. Tell 'em, Howard.

(*All look at* **HOWARD**; *he feels pressured to continue the story, in fact, any story.*)

HOWARD. Actually, I'm a…well, I'm more of a…a restaurateur.

JINKS. What a small world. So am I.

TAMMY. Howard's restaurants are just about everywhere. Isn't that true, Howard?

HOWARD. Better already.

(**HOWARD** *takes another step or two.* **CORDELIA** *assists.*)

CORDELIA. I just know I've heard your voice somewhere… Mr.…

TAMMY. Brown. Howard W. Brown. I'm Tammy Brown, of course. Nice to meet ya.

(**HOWARD** – *with* **CORDELIA**'s *continuing assistance* – *takes a few additional steps which* **HOWARD** *enjoys and* **TAMMY** *notes.*)

CORDELIA. That's better.

(*A jealous* **TAMMY** *steps quickly to* **HOWARD**, *all but pushing* **CORDELIA** *aside.*)

JINKS. So, do y'all have restaurants in these parts?

TAMMY. That's why we're here, isn't it, Howard?

HOWARD. These nice people aren't interested in –

TAMMY. Howard's the king of…well, of…chicken restaurants.

JINKS. You said they were gourmet.

TAMMY. They are! At Howard's Chicken and...Waffle World...they serve those little suckers twenty different *gourmet* ways –

HOWARD. Tammy –

TAMMY. Fried, barbecued...roasted, toasted – !

JINKS. So we're getting another chicken restaurant?

TAMMY. Shhh...it's a secret.

OLIVE. Oh, Lord, Mr. Brown. Does *she* have a promotion for you. *(points to* **JINKS***, flaps her arms like a chicken)*

*(***CORDELIA*** steps to the porch, quietly surveys the damage.)*

EMMA. The best laid plans, huh?

CORDELIA. Miz Darlington...I'm sorry.

EMMA. Your idea...it would've worked just like you said.

TAMMY. Is something wrong?

EMMA. It seems we picked the wrong day to have a gathering on the porch.

OLIVE. We had hoped to raise money...to save Old Smokey for Emma's son.

TAMMY. We'll help out there. Won't we, Howard?

EMMA. Unfortunately, the road's closed –

CORDELIA. And the power's out, so...

EMMA. So even if we could get everything fixed...the power back, the porch cleared...

TAMMY. *(she understands)* Nobody could get here.

(Silence as the women look at one another.)

I'll tell you what my mama does when things don't look so good. She prays.

OLIVE. Why didn't I think of that?

TAMMY. But I'd be honored if you'd let me lead.

HOWARD. Tammy, I need you.

TAMMY. A *short* prayer, Howard. Dear Lord... *(she sees that all but* **HOWARD** *have bowed their heads.)* Howard, it won't work unless you join us! *(she looks at* **HOWARD** *who isn't interested in praying.)* HOWARD!

(Pressured, **HOWARD** *bows his head.)*

Lord...your son was raised by a carpenter...so fixing up a porch and – while you're at it – bringing back the power and maybe opening that little old road out there...that should be right up your alley. In Thy name we pray. Amen.

OLIVE, EMMA, JINKS, CORDELIA. Amen.

(Abruptly, **HOWARD** *takes* **TAMMY**'s *hand, pulls her to the door leading to the porch. He smiles, as if that were an excuse for his action.)*

TAMMY. See y'all later...since we can't go anywhere. Not yet, anyway. (**HOWARD** *is now pulling her)* Howard...I'm coming!

*(**HOWARD** and **TAMMY** exit. As they do, we hear another gust of wind and a clap of thunder.)*

CORDELIA. I know I've heard that man's voice somewhere.

JINKS. His name is Howard W. Brown. Does that help?

CORDELIA. Maybe it isn't?

OLIVE. Cordelia's always been the suspicious member of our family.

CORDELIA. First his wife says he's a world renowned gourmet chef.

JINKS. Well, I never heard of him.

CORDELIA. Then he changes everything. Caims he owns restaurants.

OLIVE. Not only that...he's the king of chicken restaurants.

JINKS. *(facetiously)* Now *that* is royalty.

CORDELIA. If that were true, wouldn't one of us have heard of him? Or Howard's Chicken and Waffle World? Plus Brown's a name like Smith –

OLIVE. Or Jones.

CORDELIA. On top of everything...what's he doing up here...on a day like this?

OLIVE. Looking to build another restaurant maybe...?

CORDELIA. Up here? Oh, Mama. I don't think so.

EMMA. You think they've lied to us.

CORDELIA. I think they're hiding something, Miz Darlington.

OLIVE. But what?

JINKS. And why?

(The women look at one another; none has an answer.)

EMMA. So...on top of everything...we've got ourselves a mystery.

*(We hear another clap of thunder. A troubled **EMMA** looks out to the porch and the downed tree.)*

JINKS. Emma, don't worry

OLIVE. We'll save Old Smokey. Won't we, Cordelia?

CORDELIA. Well, I do have another idea –

OLIVE. Isn't she something?

CORDELIA. We'll need the power back. Telephone too. Not to mention...everybody's going to have to pitch in ...

JINKS. Of course, we'll pitch in.

CORDELIA. And while we're at it we'll figure out who this so-called Mr. Brown is –

OLIVE. And why he's here.

CORDELIA. Actually, Mama, I think I know how to do that.

*(As **CORDELIA** smiles, **EMMA** folds her arms across her chest. At the same time, we hear another crack of thunder. It's obvious the storm still rages and that **EMMA** isn't optimistic that things will work out.)*

Miz Darlington, really...something good's gonna happen.

OLIVE. I can feel it, too, Emma.

JINKS. All of us can.

CORDELIA. And it's going to happen real soon. Promise.

> (*CORDELIA's comforting words are barely out of her mouth then we see another flash of lightning and a loud clap of thunder followed by a resounding BANG. Out of sight, another tree limb has slammed Old Smokey's porch, seemingly making* **OLIVE**, **JINKS** *and* **CORDELIA**'s *promise to* **EMMA** *nothing more than a fanciful wish. As lights flicker, then go out for good, we hear a spiritual that reinforces what we've just seen, maybe an upbeat version of "Oh, Didn't It Rain."*)

End of Scene

Scene Two

(The sales area of Old Smokey, an hour or so later, enough time for the storm to have passed and for **CORDELIA** *to have worked up a little ditty we're about to hear. The candles and/or oil lamps are once again lit and the tree branch remains. In fact, a new smaller branch – no doubt the one we heard crash at the end of the previous scene – now lies alongside the first. Because power remains out, they're barely visible.)*

*(**AT RISE** – as the music we've heard during the scene change is down and out – **CORDELIA** stands in front of her microphone. She hesitates a long moment; then – just as **HOWARD** enters from the porch – she begins to sing the following words to the tune "It's A Long Way To Tipperary," all the while pretending she doesn't know **HOWARD**'s anywhere around.)*

"WE'RE HEADING TO HOWARD'S CHICKEN"

CORDELIA.
WE ARE HEADING, TO HOWARD'S CHICKEN,
ORDERING WAFFLES THERE, TOO.
WE ARE HEADING, TO HOWARD'S CHICKEN,
IT'S THE BEST AND THAT'S TRUE.

GOODBYE COLONEL SANDERS,
FAREWELL POPEYES, TOO.
WE ARE HEADING TO HOWARD'S CHICKEN…

*(**CORDELIA** now admits **HOWARD**'s presence, acting embarrassed as she sings the last verse in hesitant fashion.)*

…IT'S THE BEST…AND THAT'S TRUE.

Mr. Brown! I thought once the storm passed you'd walked down the road with Mama and the rest. I sure didn't want you to hear me.

HOWARD. Impressive.

CORDELIA. Thank you, but –

HOWARD. No, no. I recognize talent when I hear it. And beauty when I see it.

CORDELIA. When I heard you were the king of chicken – oh, I hope you don't mind me saying that – all kinds of things…music, words…popped into my head. Before I knew it I was singing into this silly microphone. Of course, we're not on the air…not yet anyway.

HOWARD. You should be.

CORDELIA. The funny thing is…I *do* have my own…real…little radio program…on a tiny little station…that nobody ever listens to probably –

HOWARD. Interesting…

CORDELIA. It's called "Cordelia In The Mornin'." But some day, Mr. Brown, I'm gonna be –

HOWARD. Call me, Howard.

CORDELIA. All right, I will. Some day, Howard…I'm gonna be on radio everywhere in America. Wouldn't that be something? And if I get real famous maybe you'll let me do a singing commercial for your chicken places…

(**HOWARD** *sings the opening line to* **CORDELIA**'s *song, again to "It's A Long Way To Tipperary."*)

HOWARD.
WE'RE HEADING TO HOWARD'S CHICKEN…

(**CORDELIA** *joins in and she and* **HOWARD** *sing in unison. They sound surprisingly good together.*)

HOWARD & CORDELIA.
…ORDERING WAFFLES THERE TOO.

(**CORDELIA** *and* **HOWARD** *share a laugh.*)

HOWARD. I believe we could be a team.

CORDELIA. What are you talking about, Howard? We already are. (**CORDELIA** *crosses her arms over her chest.*)

HOWARD. You're chilled.

CORDELIA. A little maybe.

HOWARD. Here…let me warm you up. *(places his hands on her shoulders)*

CORDELIA. I'm surprised at you, Howard! You're a married man! *(steps away from **HOWARD**)*

HOWARD. You think that… *(He's forgotten **TAMMY**'s name again.)* …woman is –

CORDELIA. Tammy. And, yes…I think she's your wife.

HOWARD. Simply my…traveling secretary.

CORDELIA. She said you were married.

HOWARD. Surely you misunderstood. *(now rubbing **CORDELIA**'s shoulders)*

CORDELIA. She also said you own a bunch of chicken restaurants. Maybe that's not true either.

HOWARD. I ask you, Cordelia…do I look like the "king of chicken"?

CORDELIA. You mean you're not?

HOWARD. Sorry to disappoint. It is Cordelia?

CORDELIA. I'm so embarrassed. I make up a silly song about Howard's Chicken World – of all the crazy things – you hear me sing it and –

HOWARD. *(determined to "comfort" **CORDELIA** or die trying)* I loved it.

CORDELIA. *(equally determined to avoid **HOWARD**'s advances)* But it didn't make any sense. And now I feel foolish. I bet your name isn't even Howard. Because I know I've heard your voice somewhere, and I don't remember hearing anybody named Howard W. Brown.

HOWARD. Have you heard of the Brown Broadcasting Company?

CORDELIA. I have not!

HOWARD. Also known as the BBC…

CORDELIA. Well…maybe I've heard of the BBC.

HOWARD. That's me, Cordelia.

CORDELIA. I am real sorry. I still don't believe a word of it.

HOWARD. *(in his best broadcast voice, with a British accent)* Ladies and gentlemen…you are listening to the BBC. Does that sound familiar?

CORDELIA. Maybe, I guess…a little.

HOWARD. Name a city. I'll own a station there…

CORDELIA. New York City.

HOWARD. Two stations.

CORDELIA. Miami, Florida.

HOWARD. One. But I'm buying another.

CORDELIA. If that's true – your name's really Howard W. Brown, you own half the radio stations in America – why are you stuck on a mountain top in the middle of a tornado with somebody who claims to be your wife but you say isn't? Trying at first to make us believe you're the chicken king of the universe?

HOWARD. I'm on the road. Do you understand what that means?

CORDELIA. I don't know…

HOWARD. I'm searching for talent…incognito.

CORDELIA. You mean for your radio stations? Oh, now I know you're fibbing me. *(turning to exit;* **HOWARD** *grabs her arm)*

HOWARD. And guess who I've got my eyes on.

CORDELIA. More than your eyes, Howard. *(she removes his hands – one at a time – from her arm)*

HOWARD. Except there's a problem…

CORDELIA. And what is that?

HOWARD. You're entirely too attractive for radio.

CORDELIA. My mama warned me about men like you.

HOWARD. You, my dear, should be seen…in living color… from coast to coast…around the world…morning, noon and night.

CORDELIA. If you're talking about TV, you can't help me, can you? Because you're in radio.

HOWARD. Television…that's also why I'm here –

CORDELIA. Oh, I know what you're gonna say. You're gonna tell me you're a big shot in TV too.

HOWARD. I am not in television –

CORDELIA. See!

HOWARD. But I will be. So you understand, Cordelia, I'm beginning slowly…in the part of the country where I can explore opportunities without paying excessively. But, then if you want to be on radio –

CORDELIA. Actually, I love television. In fact, I've always dreamed of being a TV weathergirl. "Good evening, everybody, this is Cordelia Dunwitty with your eleven p.m. weather." Tell me the truth, Howard. Does somebody really give weathergirls all those pretty little outfits they wear? *(suddenly skeptical again)* But then you don't know because right now you're only in radio. If that part's true. Which I don't think it is.

HOWARD. Cordelia…

CORDELIA. What?

HOWARD. I can change your life. *(once again approaching* **CORDELIA***)*

CORDELIA. Howard…things like that don't happen.

HOWARD. For people I like and who like me… *(looking into* **CORDELIA***'s eyes, very dramatic, as if he might be saying it on radio)* I have the *power*…to make dreams come true.

(**HOWARD** *no more says the word "power" then the electrical power inside Old Smokey returns. In the light, we can see* **CORDELIA** *has a sudden realization, based on what* **HOWARD** *has said and how he's said it.*)

CORDELIA. *I know who you are – !*

(Before **CORDELIA** *can identify* **HOWARD**, *he makes his move on her, taking her into his arms. At the very same moment,* **TAMMY** *enters.)*

TAMMY. *HOWARD! WHAT DO YOU THINK YOU'RE DOING?*

*(***TAMMY** – *her hands on her hips – stares at* **HOWARD** *while he and* **CORDELIA** *freeze. After a moment,* **TAMMY** *storms from the stage and runs down the aisle.* **HOWARD** *follows, shouting to her as does.)*

HOWARD. *ANNIE!*

TAMMY. *(angrily correcting* **HOWARD** *without looking back) TAMMY!*

*(***TAMMY,** *followed by* **HOWARD,** *disappears into the dark.)*

End of Scene

Scene Three

(Old Smokey. A couple of hours have passed. Electrical power is still on, but the road remains closed. In addition to the guitar seen in previous scenes, there's a basket containing additional instruments, including musical spoons, washboard, triangle, etc.)

(AT RISE, CORDELIA stands in front of the microphone. To one ear she holds the kind of headphones you'd find in a radio studio. EMMA, OLIVE and JINKS gather around. At the same time, we see TAMMY and HOWARD on the porch; she's removing the tree limbs while he watches.)

CORDELIA. *(speaking into the mike, nervously)* Test...test...

OLIVE. *(whispering while looking at HOWARD on the porch)* So, what's he doing here, Cordelia?

CORDELIA. I told you. I don't know.

OLIVE. If you're right, he's a very famous man.

CORDELIA. Mama, I'm right! And we'll find out why he's here.

JINKS. So...standing out there, we've got the one and only –

CORDELIA. *Shhh! (listening via the earphones, then speaking into the mike)* Sixty seconds. Got ya. *(to the women)* Now, are we gonna save Old Smokey or what?

OLIVE. What do you want us to do?

CORDELIA. I told you. I even wrote some of it out for you.

EMMA. But a "Saturday Night at Old Smokey"...*on the radio*...I don't know...

OLIVE. The road's still closed, so –

CORDELIA. So it's this or nothing, Miz Darlington. I'm sorry, but it is.

JINKS. Look at it this way, Emma...the power *did* come back –

OLIVE. And the telephone's finally working –

CORDELIA. Both of which we'll need if we're going pull this off.

EMMA. So…maybe somebody a whole lot bigger than… *(looks at* **HOWARD***)* is telling us this *is* going to work.

*(***HOWARD*** and* **TAMMY*** abruptly enter from the porch.* **TAMMY*** senses that* **CORDELIA***'s still a tad embarrassed about* **HOWARD***'s advances.)*

TAMMY. Oh, honey, I *know* you weren't encouraging him when I walked in on y'all. He's a man…he can't help it. *(critically)* Isn't that right, Howard?

HOWARD. *(notes the headphones, etc.)* What's this…?

CORDELIA. Radio, Mr. Brown. But then you know all about radio. *(looks at her watch)* Fifteen seconds. And I'm counting on you being a part of our little show.

HOWARD. I don't think so.

CORDELIA. *(smiles at* **HOWARD** *as if to say, "Your time will come")* Now…if I only knew what I was going to do…

(Takes a deep breath, picks up the guitar, then speaks into the microphone with a sense of dramatics and folksiness we haven't heard from her before)

HELLO, EAST TENNESSEE! Welcome to…W-R-E-T Radio's first ever…SATURDAY NIGHT AT OLD SMOKEY!

*(***CORDELIA** *– the guitar still in hand – plays a slowed-down version of "She'll Be Comin' 'Round The Mountain." After a bar or two, she sings the following to the music.)*

"OH, WE ARE LIVE FROM OLD SMOKEY, YES WE ARE"

CORDELIA.
OH, WE ARE LIVE FROM OLD SMOKEY, YES WE ARE.
OH, WE ARE LIVE FROM OLD SMOKEY, YES WE ARE.
THERE'LL BE SONG, TALK AND JIVE.
WHILE WE'RE BROADCASTING LIVE.
WE ARE LIVE FROM OLD SMOKEY, YES WE ARE (YES, MA'AM!)

CORDELIA. *(stops singing, into the mike)* Tonight we're coming to you – yes, live! – from Old Smokey Country Store which just happens to be nestled on the highest mountain this side of Knoxville. Old timers will remember Old Smokey for lots more than beans, corn meal, and the best view in Johnson County. The porch out front was where y'all celebrated on Saturday nights. I'm told the hooting and hollering…the singin', the fiddlin'… could be heard all the way to Nashville.

*(***CORDELIA*** looks at ***JINKS***. With the help of a sheet of paper which ***EMMA*** may hold up for her, ***JINKS*** picks up a tambourine and sings the words as ***TAMMY*** strums the tune on her guitar.)*

JINKS.
WE'LL BE PLAYING COUNTY MUSIC, COME ON UP.
WE'LL BE PLAYING COUNTRY MUSIC, COME ON UP.
THERE'LL BE SINGIN' AND SOME PICKIN',
GET YOUR BOOTS ON, THEY'LL BE KICKIN'.
WE'LL BE PLAYING COUNTRY MUSIC, COME ON UP (SEE YOU SOON!)

CORDELIA. *(again into the mike)* We had planned to bring it all back just like you remembered. We hoped y'all would come up, celebrate with us. Unfortunately, that nasty little storm – we do hope y'all are all right and your homes are safe – closed the road leading up here. So while we're stuck, we're doing the next best thing… we're gathering 'round the old pot belly stove that's seen a lot of pickin' through the years…musical instruments at our side. Before you can say, "I love old-time country and gospel music," we'll be singing and playing some of your favorites. Why? Because Old Smokey – an "institution" in our little corner of the world for over sixty years – is threatened. That's right! The folks at the courthouse are telling us that unless taxes are paid by Monday morning, the store that helped feed your families and entertain your souls not only won't reopen, it'll be gone forever. *So…*

(**CORDELIA** *looks at* **OLIVE**, *expecting her to sing; with the help of words on paper, she does.*)

OLIVE.
WE'LL BE SAVING OLD SMOKEY, YES WE WILL.
WE'LL BE SAVING OLD SMOKEY, YES WE WILL.
CALL YOUR FRIENDS, CALL YOUR HONEY,
YOU'LL BE DONATING MONEY.
WE'LL BE SAVING OLD SMOKEY, YES WE WILL (ALL RIGHT!)

CORDELIA. There's lots more at risk. Which we'll talk about later…including how you can help make this old place bigger and better than ever. Right now, all you need to know is… *(singing and playing again, with added enthusiasm)*
IT'S SATURDAY NIGHT AT OLD SMOKEY, YES IT IS!

(**CORDELIA** *nods to* **OLIVE** *and* **JINKS**, *inviting both to join in.* **JINKS** *does which is enough to keep* **OLIVE** *from doing so. This is not to say that from time to time – as motivated by their character – each of the women, including* **TAMMY**, *doesn't select an instrument from the basket and join in the festivities.*)

CORDELIA & JINKS.
IT'S SATURDAY NIGHT AT OLD SMOKEY, YES IT IS!
SATURDAY NIGHT AND IT'S FINE.
GRAB YOUR BEER, GRAB YOUR WINE.

(**OLIVE** *raises her eyebrows to the reference to beer and wine.*)

IT'S SATURDAY NIGHT AT OLD SMOKEY, YES IT IS (HEE HAW!)

CORDELIA. Now, that you know what we're planning…I'll introduce the folks who'll make it happen. *(looks at* **OLIVE***)* Mama, tell 'em something about yourself. Of course, I'm talking about my mama, Olive Dunwitty….

(**CORDELIA** *looks at* **OLIVE**, *applauding as she does.* **EMMA**, **TAMMY** *and maybe even* **JINKS** *[less enthusiastically, of course] join in. Unfortunately,* **OLIVE** *has no idea what to say and doesn't move.*)

CORDELIA. For the first time ever, the cat's got Mama's tongue. Mama – in addition to being the best mama in the world – sings up a storm at the Fairview Free-Will Baptist Church…two services Sunday mornings, prayer services Wednesday evenings. Not only that, but once-upon-a time she was half of a really big-time singing duet called the "Mountain Mamas." I'm talking about a long time ago. How many years ago, Mama?

OLIVE. I can't count that high, Cordelia.

CORDELIA. The exciting thing is, this evening we have the other half of the fabulous singing "Mamas" with us… Miz Jinks Wilkins. Now, we're still calling them "the Mamas" even though Miz Wilkins isn't married –

JINKS. Not yet!

OLIVE. And Elvis lives.

CORDELIA. *(sneers at her mother)* What Miz Wilkins is, is an entrepreneur. She's run a bunch of different businesses, including one that's coming your way real soon…a fancy new gourmet restaurant downtown… corner of Fifth and Main, across from Homer's Feed Store and Hatchery. So y'all come by and get a free appetizer – at the gourmet restaurant, of course. Isn't that right, Miz Wilkins?

*(A surprised **JINKS** nods her head because she feels she has to. At the same time, **CORDELIA** crosses her fingers, holds her hand up.)*

If we were on TV, you'd see my fingers are crossed because I'm hoping the "Mountain Mamas" who – in case you didn't know – have been feuding over silly stuff way too long – will sing together one more time.

*(In unison, **OLIVE** and **JINKS** shake their heads.)*

Would you look at that? They've just signaled they can't wait to reprise their big hit from way back when.

*(**OLIVE** and **JINKS** can't believe **CORDELIA** has committed them to doing something they'd rather die than do.)*

CORDELIA. Before that happens, however, I've got more folks to introduce, starting with Miz Emma Darlington whose family opened Old Smokey before most of us were born. I've been told, Miz Darlington, lots of interesting things have happened up here. Is that true?

EMMA. You're talking about the night when you-know-who ended up here...

CORDELIA. Yes, Ma'am. And we'd love if you'd share it with us...

*(A reluctant **EMMA** joins **CORDELIA** at the mike.)*

EMMA. As long as everybody listening knows I do ladies' hair lots better than tell stories on radio. *(pauses, collects her thoughts)* It was August 19, 1972. I remember because it was my eleventh birthday. Oh, Lord...I think I've just told everybody how old I am. But that's okay because it was a special night that began like all the other Saturday Nights at Old Smokey...my daddy on the porch, playing his fiddle, as old cars and pickups filled the lot. Before it was full dark, a shiny new Cadillac drove up. I figured whoever was driving it wasn't from around here. I found out I was right when a nice-looking man – a fiddle in hand – stepped from the car, walked up to Daddy, whispered in his ear... causing Daddy to all but die on the spot. If he had, he would've gone with a smile on his face. And it would've been Mr. Acuff's fault –

CORDELIA. That's Roy Acuff, of course...the King of Country Music ...

EMMA. From up the road in Fountain City. It seems he was returning to Nashville and decided to look us up. In a wink he was playing his hits, including *"Wabash Cannon Ball,"* everybody clapping and carrying on. But it was what he did next that I remember. He called me to the porch...showed me a yo-yo...asked if I knew how it worked. I had no idea, but I didn't tell him that. Next thing I knew, he was making it do everything but sing...

after which he got around to teaching me to at least make it hum a little. What I didn't know, Cordelia, was that that same Mr. Acuff had shown President Richard Nixon how to do those tricks a few months earlier…on the stage of the Grand Ole Opry. So, the way I've got it figured – because of that night – Old Smokey's got something in common with the Opry…*and* I've had the honor of being taught by a teacher of a President of the United States. Now…that's my story. *(smiles, quickly steps from the mike)*

CORDELIA. A wonderful one, Miz Darlington. Thank you. *(applauds* **EMMA***'s effort)* Also alongside are Tammy and Howard W. Brown who've come a long way to be with us this evening. *(turning to* **HOWARD** *and* **TAMMY***)* Now, where do y'all call home…?

TAMMY.	**HOWARD.**
(enthusiastically)	*(reluctantly, softly)*
Kentucky.	North Carolina.

CORDELIA. I believe they're telling us they've got more than one home. I'm not surprised 'cause Howard's a big entrepreneur. Would you listen to that? Thanks to you, Mr. Brown…I've now said that ten-dollar word twice, on the radio no less…in a Southern accent. He owns restaurants and radio stations, and I've got the inside scoop…he's wants to buy a TV station in our neck of the woods. If you've got one for sale, y'all know who to call.

(The new information adds to **TAMMY***'s growing concern regarding* **HOWARD** *who glares at* **CORDELIA***.)*

Truth be told, Mr. Brown's never met a microphone he didn't love. So, if he'd kindly join me up here…

*(***EMMA** *and the other women clap as* **HOWARD** *– who truly can't resist saying something – steps to the mike.)*

HOWARD. Hello… *(turning to the women, sarcastically)* East Tennessee.

(CORDELIA stares critically at HOWARD as he smiles, steps from the mike. At the same time, TAMMY points to herself, indicating she'd liked to be included in the proceedings.)

CORDELIA. It looks like Tammy wants to be part of our show. I'm thinking we're in for a special treat.

(That's all the motivation TAMMY needs to step to the microphone. As she does, EMMA, OLIVE, JINKS and CORDELIA applaud.)

TAMMY. *(speaking into the microphone, sweetly in contrast to HOWARD's radio greeting)* Hello, East Tennessee. And, Mama, if you're listening up in the hills of Kentucky, this is for you.

(She hums an appropriate upbeat song, then proceeds to dance a step or two to the beat, stops, then again speaks into the mike.)

Oh, I do hope y'all enjoy it …

(TAMMY resumes her humming and dancing, perhaps nothing more than a pom-pom or baton routine [without the pom-poms or batons, of course]. Whatever it is, it's over-the-top as well as visibly entertaining but not something for radio and certainly not what CORDELIA had expected. CORDELIA allows TAMMY to do her thing for a long moment, then hurries back to the microphone. She speaks as TAMMY hums, dances, pretends to throw batons, etc.)

CORDELIA. I ask you…where is television when you need it? I mean, here in front of us we are seeing – some of us are seeing – the most original dancing performance ever. Something like…well, like…a Dallas Cowboy cheerleader meets the Grand Old Opry.

(TAMMY, now encouraged, picks up the beat.)

Too bad we're on radio.

*(Abruptly, **TAMMY** stops dancing; it is as if she had forgotten the radio part and is embarrassed.)*

TAMMY. I am so sorry –

CORDELIA. No, no. It was real good –

TAMMY. *(rushing back to the microphone)* For a minute I was thinking I was on television again. *(thinks about what she's said, after which it's confession time)* Except I've never been on television. Unless you call being in the Miss Bituminous Coal beauty contest – standing next to the girl who won – being on television. Which doesn't mean I haven't dreamed of being on big-time TV. Or in the movies. In fact, every night I close my eyes… and there I am…in Technicolor on the biggest screen you've ever seen looking into some big movie star's blue eyes. He's telling me I'm prettier and more talented than I ever imagined. And the wonderful thing is…*it's gonna happen!* That's true, isn't it, Howard?

*(**HOWARD** looks away, giving **TAMMY** another hint that all may not be as she had hoped.)*

So, if you're listening to me out there – including you, Mama – please come to see me at a theatre near you. Assuming I'm really gonna be at a…theatre near you.

*(As a comfort to **TAMMY**, immediately **CORDELIA** begins to sing an a cappella version of "Down To The River To Pray.")*

"DOWN TO THE RIVER TO PRAY"

CORDELIA.
AS I WENT DOWN TO THE RIVER TO PRAY,
STUDYING ABOUT THAT GOOD OL' WAY
AND WHO WILL WEAR THE STARRING CROWN?
GOOD LORD, SHOW ME THE WAY!

*(**CORDELIA** encourages **EMMA**, **JINKS** and **OLIVE** to sing the refrain. Realizing **JINKS** will in fact sing, **OLIVE** again refuses.)*

EMMA & JINKS.
> O SISTERS, LET'S GO DOWN,
> LET'S GO DOWN, COME ON DOWN.
> O SISTERS, LET'S GO DOWN,
> DOWN TO THE RIVER TO PRAY.

CORDELIA.
> AS I WENT DOWN TO THE RIVER TO PRAY,
> STUDYING ABOUT THAT GOOD OL' WAY
> AND WHO WILL WEAR THE STARRING CROWN?
> GOOD LORD, SHOW ME THE WAY!

> Normally, a hymn's included at the end of something. But I've been told – thank you, Mama – there's never a bad time to praise the Lord. *(pauses, not sure what to do next)* Now…where were we…?

JINKS. If we're allowed to do commercials, I've got something to say.

CORDELIA. I ask you, Miz Wilkins…what's radio without advertising?

JINKS. *(stepping to the mike)* Good. Because I want to talk about The Cats' Meow.

CORDELIA. That's Miz Darlington's beauty shop, of course. Downtown, across from the courthouse –

JINKS. A testimonial, really.

OLIVE. *(rushing to **JINKS**, not to be outdone)* Now, hold your horses. I am also a loyal customer of the Cats' Meow –

JINKS. *(quickly, into the mike, almost as an announcement)* The Cat's Meow…"Where A Mirror Is Your Friend."

OLIVE. *(hoping to upstage **JINKS**)* The Cat's Meow…"Where Age Never Wins."

JINKS. Well, I go more than you do.

OLIVE. 'Cause you need it a hell of a lot more!

CORDELIA. Mama!

OLIVE. It's true, Cordelia! And I don't care who knows!

CORDELIA. *(again for the benefit of the radio audience)* Now, I told y'all they like to fuss at one another.

OLIVE. I'm in and out in a wink. And if I say so myself, looking like a million dollars. While Emma slaves over her... *(points to* **JINKS***)* ...half the day.

JINKS. Now you've gone too far.

CORDELIA. Miz Wilkins, this isn't the place –

JINKS. Your mama, Cordelia, has a mustache –

OLIVE. *How dare you!*

JINKS. But you probably never noticed, *because she has it bleached* –

OLIVE. *Why you...!*

JINKS. *At the Cats' Meow...every Thursday morning...rain or shine...come hell or high water* –

(**EMMA** *steps between* **JINKS** *and* **OLIVE** *who immediately shields her alleged "mustache" from view. As she does,* **CORDELIA** *sings an a cappella version of "Go Tell It On The Mountain."*)

"GO TELL IT ON THE MOUNTAIN"

CORDELIA.
GO TELL IT ON THE MOUNTAIN,
OVER THE HILLS AND EVERYWHERE.
GO TELL IT ON THE MOUNTAIN,
THAT JESUS CHRIST IS BORN.

Sing with me, Mama!

(*An upset* **OLIVE** *joins in the singing of the hymn all the while continuing to hold her hand to her face in a continuing effort to hide the supposed mustache.*)

CORDELIA & OLIVE.
WHILE SHEPHERDS KEPT THEIR WATCHING,
O'ER SILENT FLOCKS BY NIGHT,
BEHOLD THROUGHOUT THE HEAVENS,
THERE SHONE A HOLY LIGHT...*SO*

GO TELL IT ON THE MOUNTAIN,
OVER THE HILLS AND EVERYWHERE.
GO TELL IT ON THE MOUNTAIN,
THAT JESUS CHRIST IS BORN!

CORDELIA. At times like this, one gospel just isn't enough. Especially when we've got a special one that celebrates our mountain heritage during the upcoming season of... *(looking critically at* **JINKS** *and* **OLIVE**) *...peace on earth and good will toward EVERYBODY! (pauses)* Now... as some of you may know, I'm about to become a bride. Oh, I can hear all the young men out there crying in their Mountain Dews. This fall I'll proudly walk down the aisle with Lance Corporal Theodore Benjamin Darlington – we call him Teddy – who just happens to be Miz Darlington's son and who's coming home on Friday. Get out those welcome signs! In addition to loving him to pieces, we're both very proud of him...he's been serving his country somewhere I don't think any of us would want to go...Afghanistan. I debated whether I should tell y'all the rest of the story. I decided I would. Except I don't want anybody feeling sorry for him. There's no time for that because, before we know it, the nasty effects of the bomb he got too close to will be gone. Till then, Miz Darlington thinks – and his doctors do too – that he'll need a special place like Old Smokey to help get his feet back on the ground. If that's gonna happen...if this little store at the top of the mountain that Teddy loves like you can't imagine is to be around for another six days or sixty years...it's gonna take a little help from you. That means...working together we're...

(**CORDELIA** *nods to* **EMMA** *and* **OLIVE** *who join* **CORDELIA** *at the mike. Together they clap and sing the following to the tune of "Down By The Riverside."* **CORDELIA** *joins in on a guitar.*)

"UP ON THE MOUNTAIN SIDE"

CORDELIA, EMMA & OLIVE.
GONNA HELP SAVE OLD SMOKEY NOW,
UP ON THE MOUNTAIN SIDE,
UP ON THE MOUNTAIN SIDE,
UP ON THE MOUNTAIN SIDE.
GONNA HELP SAVE OLD SMOKEY NOW.
UP ON THE MOUNTAIN SIDE.

(EMMA and OLIVE softly repeat an a cappella version of the song's refrain as CORDELIA speaks into the microphone.)

EMMA & OLIVE.
WE AIN'T GONNA WAIT TILL IT'S TOO LATE,
WE AIN'T GONNA WAIT TILL IT'S TOO LATE.
SAVE OLD SMOKEY NOW.
WE AIN'T GONNA WAIT TILL IT'S TOO LATE,
WE AIN'T GONNA WAIT TILL IT'S TOO LATE.
SAVE OLD SMOKEY NOW.

CORDELIA. If you haven't guessed it, that's our commercial for the evening. Which also means we're sending you back to the station. They'll tell you how you can help us do just that...save Old Smokey for Teddy and generations to come. So dig out those checkbooks...grab loose change if that's all you've got...take it down to the Dunwitty Funeral Home. Daddy'll make sure it's at the courthouse in time. Then tell everybody to tune in. 'Cause it's *"Saturday Night at Old Smokey"* and –

(EMMA steps to the microphone. OLIVE stops singing.)

EMMA. May I say something, Cordelia?

(CORDELIA nods, steps back from the mike.)

Cordelia would tell you I had planned to do this by myself, with help from my friends, two of whom keep promising to behave themselves. *(eyes JINKS and OLIVE)* We'd reopen Old Smokey...pay off what's owed from the sales we made. But I'm old enough to know when something I want more than anything isn't gonna happen. So, if you're willing to help and Old Smokey's saved...y'all are invited to the grandest reopening celebration ever...offering good old country entertainment, plus the best nibbles in Johnson County.

JINKS. *(into the microphone)* Including a *very* special...deep-south hummus.

EMMA. What's important is...God bless y'all for helping.

CORDELIA. *(applauding* **EMMA**'s *offer)* We've got lots more music – plus a big-time surprise – coming your way. So, nobody go away.

(**EMMA** *and* **CORDELIA** *join* **OLIVE** *in a chorus of "Up On The Mountainside." After a moment,* **CORDELIA** *steps away from the mike.* **EMMA** *crosses to* **CORDELIA**, *gives her a hug.)*

What's that for?

EMMA. Everything! Especially the things you said about Teddy.

OLIVE. Plus you were wonderful, Cordelia.

CORDELIA. We'll talk about that when we know how much we've raised. Right now, we've got business. *(looks at* **TAMMY**, *crosses to her, takes her hand, caringly)* Tammy, I think you know what I'm gonna say. Whoever Howard told you he was –

TAMMY. A big-time movie producer. But you're not a big-time movie-anything, are you, Howard?

CORDELIA. For sure, his last name isn't Brown.

TAMMY. *(to* **HOWARD***)* How could you lie to me like that?

CORDELIA. He lied to me too.

TAMMY. You didn't believe him.

CORDELIA. I wanted to. Because he told me…like he told you and who knows how many other women…things we wanted to hear.

TAMMY. *(to* **HOWARD** *who remains seated)* So who are you… really?

HOWARD. I will not sit here and listen to this nonsense.

CORDELIA. *Then, Howie Hawk*…stand up.

(**HOWARD** *stands up;* **TAMMY** *hasn't a clue who he is.)*

EMMA. He's on radio, Tammy –

OLIVE. He tells everybody what to believe, how to live, who to vote for. Don't you, Mr. Hawk?

CORDELIA. And he's married.

TAMMY. *Wait till I talk to her!*

CORDELIA. The only thing we don't know is why he's here.

TAMMY. He wants Old Smokey.

EMMA. *He's* the one who tried to buy it!

CORDELIA. And when you refused, he got the county to foreclose.

OLIVE. Why you're nothing but a damn Yankee carpetbagger!

JINKS. Who tells everybody he's this great American patriot.

OLIVE. All the while trying to take something that's been in Emma's family for generations –

EMMA. That's Teddy's best chance at recovery. Shame on you, Mr. Hawk!

JINKS. Why does he want it?

TAMMY. Because he wants to film the *new "Gone With The Wind"* here.

HOWARD. Because I planned to do something on this mountain top beyond anybody's else imagination. Something to put this hay seed county on the map of the civilized world.

TAMMY. I was gonna be the new Scarlett O'Hara.

HOWARD. How could you imagine that? *(laughs)* Oh, I'm not talking about making a movie…I'm talking about expanding my broadcasting empire…high on this mountain…a transmitter so powerful my voice will be heard a half a world away. When I tell my audience of millions…"my brilliance is from on *high*"…they'll understand. *(he smiles, then crosses to exit)*

CORDELIA. A reminder, Mr. Hawk…the road's still closed.

*(***HOWARD** *remains determined to exit.)*

TAMMY. Plus there are bears out there.

(Abruptly, **HOWARD** *changes his mind.)*

JINKS. Lord, do we have a story to tell.

CORDELIA. And a radio program to tell it on.

HOWARD. *(after a moment, then laughing)* All right. You win. I'll pay the fool taxes. Old Smokey, such as it is, will be saved. Ten thousand…that should do it. Of course, it will.

> (**HOWARD** *removes a checkbook from his pocket, writes a check. All look at* **EMMA**, *waiting for her to respond. She doesn't.*)

Forget I was here. Forget I had anything to do with this woman. Forget that I was about to turn this nothingness. *(tears out the check, offers the check to* **EMMA***)*

EMMA. *(interrupting)* It's not nothingness, Mr. Hawk.

HOWARD. Oh, but it is. Always was…always will be.

> *(After a moment,* **EMMA** *accepts the check.* **HOWARD** *is suddenly at ease. He smiles broadly.)*

Now, I believe I'll just sit here. Watch the little broadcast I just bought.

> *(Abruptly,* **CORDELIA** *looks at her watch, then returns to the microphone, anxiously.)*

CORDELIA. Mama, you know *"Wabash Cannon Ball"*…sing it with me.

> (**CORDELIA** *plays the opening cords of "Wabash Cannon Ball" after which she and* **OLIVE** *sing a rousing version of the song into the mike.*)

"WABASH CANNON BALL"

CORDELIA & OLIVE.
> NOW LISTEN TO THE JINGLE,
> THE RUMBLE AND THE ROAR,
> AS SHE GLIDES ALONG THE WOODLANDS,
> THROUGH THE HILLS AND BY THE SHORES.
>
> HEAR THE MIGHTY RUSH OF ENGINES,
> HEAR THE LONESOME HOBOS' CALL,
> WE'RE TRAVELING THROUGH THE JUNGLES
> ON THE WABASH CANNON BALL.

CORDELIA. With a bit of a Roy Acuff classic, welcome back to "Saturday Night at Old Smokey." Standing here, ready to sing, are the "Mountain Mamas." Just part of what we've planned to entertain and…maybe inform. *(looks at* **EMMA***, hoping she'll reconsider accepting the check)* Hearing that little exchange between my mama and Miz Wilkins, I'm betting you're saying there's no way Cordelia's gonna get them up here to sing together. What you don't know is that's how they entertain themselves. They even keep score. And after all these years, they're just about even. So, what better time to hear 'em again? *The "Mountain Mamas," everybody…*

(Applauding, **CORDELIA** *looks at* **JINKS** *and* **OLIVE** *who shake their heads in unison. As they do,* **TAMMY** *steps to the mike.)*

TAMMY. I know I'm interrupting. But I've got something to say.

*(***CORDELIA** *steps away. It's obvious* **TAMMY** *doesn't know how to say what it is she needs to say. She takes a moment to gather herself and speaks.)*

Mama, remember when I was little? You'd tuck me in, read me a fairy tale till I fell asleep. Except for that special one I stayed awake to hear 'cause I loved how it ended. Once upon a time there was a girl who didn't have fancy clothes and nobody thought was pretty. Then – overnight almost – she got discovered by a handsome prince. Like magic, her dreams came true, and she lived happily ever after. Well, like Cinderella … I'm been looking, Mama. Waiting tables for nickels and dimes and looking. Praying hard that my own handsome prince would walk through the door. The slipper would fit and in a wink all the ordinary things in my life would be gone. Oh, I know…the Bible tells us wanting something that bad is wrong. But like nobody you know I want to feel important. I'm hearing you, Mama…you're saying, "Hush, Tammy, you're doing it again…embarrassing yourself." Except this time I know it, and I don't care, 'cause I'm mad at myself for being so stupid to fall for his crazy stories. Ashamed I didn't tell these nice people what he was up to. Furious at him for making me feel like the fool I am. So, I'm doing two things, Mama. I'm coming home… going back to school like you told me I should. *(looks at* **HOWARD**, *who looks away)* And I'm getting even! Oh, I know that's wrong too. But if you're hearing me, lots of other folks are too. So this is my chance…it's now or never. Except I can't…'cause… *(now looks at* **EMMA** *and the check, then quickly steps away from the mike)* I can't.

*(***TAMMY*** is comforted by* **JINKS** *and* **CORDELIA**. *At the same time,* **OLIVE** *can't resist singing her favorite hymn, "Softly and Tenderly," believing it will comfort* **TAMMY**. *As she sings a cappella,* **OLIVE** *takes* **TAMMY***'s hand in hers.)*

"SOFTLY AND TENDERLY"

OLIVE.
SOFTLY AND TENDERLY, JESUS IS CALLING,
CALLING FOR YOU AND FOR ME.
SEE, ON THE PORTALS, HE'S WAITING AND WATCHING,

WATCHING FOR YOU AND FOR ME.
COME HOME, COME HOME,
YOU WHO ARE WEARY, JESUS IS CALLING…
CALLING…

(looking at **HOWARD**, *the real "sinner" in her mind)*

OH, SINNER, COME HOME!"

EMMA. *(steps to the mike, signaling to* **TAMMY** *to join her. She does.)* Stand with me, Tammy…I need all the help I can get. A couple minutes ago – before we went back on the air – I had a chance to save Old Smokey without getting y'all involved. When Teddy comes home on Friday – thank you, Lord! – there'd be no doubt he'd have a place to get his mind off the war, help him heal, focus on what's important…family and friends and Cordelia. Oh, he loves you, Cordelia, like you can't imagine! How easy it would've been to have accepted that offer in the form of the check I'm holding. All I'd have to do is keep my mouth shut...like you just did, Tammy... *(looks at* **TAMMY** *who nods her head)* Pretend somebody didn't enter our lives full of stories and lies, working behind our backs – using deception and influence – to claim Old Smokey for his own selfish purposes, never caring that this "nothingness" – that's what he called it – is what Teddy and so many others have fought and died for. Well, it won't work. Because down here, we play by the rules. We don't make fools of other folks. We don't think we're better than somebody else because we believe we have all the answers. Most of all, we don't have a radio program that's made us rich, makes us think we're something special when we're not. If you haven't guessed, I'm talking about the famous Mr. Howie Hawk who some of you may even listen to. Right now he's standing here – his mouth shut like it never is. He's looking at me.

(Looks at **HOWARD** *– his mouth shut – who appears amazed that somebody would challenge his might.)*

Thinking I'm crazy to refuse his offer. Well, Mr. Hawk, you may be powerful on radio, telling folks how great you are, spreading ignorance and hate. But down here a person's no better than his word and his reputation. And knowing what we do about you – *including that you cheat on your wife* – neither of yours is worth a hoot.

*(***EMMA*** holds the check in front of the mike, then ceremoniously tears it into a dozen pieces.* **HOWARD** *immediately places his hand over the mike to keep his words from being broadcast; he speaks softly but angrily.)*

HOWARD. Fools...all of you! Monday morning I'll tell listeners these were lies from half-wits out to destroy me, destroy America. *(laughs sarcastically)*

*(***CORDELIA*** picks up the earphones. She frowns, looks at* **HOWARD** *who continues to stand near the mike.)*

CORDELIA. We never went back on the air.

TAMMY. **OLIVE.**
No! Are you sure, Cordelia?

JINKS. Nobody heard Emma?

HOWARD. *(laughing, full of himself again)* Just what I'd expect from a bunch of country bumpkins! Oh, don't look so disappointed that your incrimination didn't leave this room…it makes not an iota of difference. The power of my voice…my unique gift to convince others of my infallibility…in the face of hearsay…is legendary.

CORDELIA. It makes no difference that you've cheated on your wife –

(**HOWARD** *looks at* **TAMMY**, *laughs again*)

TAMMY. Well, you did!

HOWARD. My dear, Tammy or whatever your name is, count yourself among scores of others. No pun intended.

CORDELIA. Plus you lied about who you were.

HOWARD. No, no, please…I admit it…I deceived. I lied. I cheated. But what's important is – like always – I've won!

(**CORDELIA** *picks up her headphones. She listens before speaking.*)

CORDELIA. I believe this country bumpkin's made a terrible mistake. We *are* on the air –

TAMMY. Including when he admitted he'd deceived, lied and cheated?

CORDELIA. Loud and clear. And in his own words. So sorry, Mr. Hawk…

TAMMY. Oh, Mama, I do hope you were listening.

(**HOWARD** *turns and storms out of Old Smokey. The women celebrate, particularly* **OLIVE** *and* **JINKS** *who hug one another until they realize what they're doing.* **CORDELIA** *steps back to the mike.*)

CORDELIA. I hope you'll excuse our little Saturday night soap opera…courtesy of the once popular, Mr. Howie Hawk. Y'all tune in to his show Monday morning – assuming he has a show – hear him try to get out of this one. To celebrate I'd like to sing one of my favorite songs…one that tells you how we're feeling…

"WE SHALL RISE"

(Sings and plays the following in a celebratory fashion)

CORDELIA.
> IN THE RESURRECTION MORNING
> WHEN THE TRUMP OF GOD SHALL RISE
> WE SHALL RISE! (HALLELUJAH!) WE SHALL RISE!
> THEN THE SAINTS WILL COME REJOICING
> AND NO TEARS WILL BE FOUND.
> WE SHALL RISE! (HALLELUJAH!) WE SHALL RISE!

*(An inspired **TAMMY** joins **CORDELIA** in the chorus.)*

CORDELIA & TAMMY.
> WE SHALL RISE! (HALLELUJAH!) WE SHALL RISE! (AMEN!)
> WE SHALL RISE! (HALLELUJAH!)
> WHEN DEATH'S PRISON BARS ARE BROKEN
> WE SHALL RISE! (HALLELUJAH!) WE SHALL RISE!

CORDELIA.
> IN THE RESURRECTION MORNING
> WHAT A MEETING IT WILL BE
> WE SHALL RISE! (HALLELUJAH!) WE SHALL RISE!
> WHEN OUR FATHERS AND OUR MOTHERS
> AND OUR LOVED ONES WE SHALL SEE.
> WE SHALL RISE! (HALLELUJAH!) WE SHALL RISE!

*(Unable to resist, **EMMA**, **OLIVE**, **TAMMY** and **JINKS** join in.)*

> WE SHALL RISE! (HALLELUJAH!) WE SHALL RISE! (AMEN!)
> WE SHALL RISE! (HALLELUJAH!)
> WHEN DEATH'S PRISON BARS ARE BROKEN
> WE SHALL RISE! (HALLELUJAH!) WE SHALL RISE!

Would you believe my Mama and Miz Wilkins are standing here…*together*? What better time to here them sing *together*? The "Mountain Mamas" everybody…

JINKS. *(to* **OLIVE***)* For old time's sake maybe?

OLIVE. I don't know. *Unless* you'll sing one of *my* favorites.

*(***EMMA** *eyes* **JINKS**. **JINKS** *gets the message.)*

JINKS. Well…I suppose it won't kill me.

*(***JINKS** *sings the opening words of the "Mountain Mama's" big hit, "Jordan Is A Hard Road To Travel.")*

"JORDAN IS A HARD ROAD TO TRAVEL"

JINKS.
> I'M GONNA SING YOU A BRAND NEW SONG,
> IT'S ALL THE TRUTH FOR CERTAIN;

*(***JINKS** *signals to* **OLIVE** *that she expects her to join her in song. A reluctant* **OLIVE** *– also motivated by* **EMMA***'s look – does and they sing together.)*

OLIVE & JINKS.
> WE CAN'T LIVE HIGH BUT WE CAN GET BY
> AND GET ON THE OTHER SIDE OF JORDAN.

*(***OLIVE** *makes an effort to step away from the mike, that is until* **JINKS** *grabs her arm. Together they sing, and – in time – even* **OLIVE** *gets into it.* **EMMA** *and* **TAMMY** *clap along with the music.)*

OLIVE & JINKS.
> OH, PULL OFF YOUR OVERCOAT AND ROLL UP YOUR SLEEVES,
> JORDAN IS A HARD ROAD TO TRAVEL;
> PULL OFF YOUR OVERCOAT AND ROLL UP YOUR SLEEVES,
> JORDAN IS A HARD ROAD TO TRAVEL, I BELIEVE.

OLIVE & JINKS.
> RAIN FORTY NIGHT, GONNA RAIN FORTY DAYS,
> GONNA RAIN IN THE *APPALACHIAN MOUNTAINS*;
> GONNA RAIN FORTY HORSES AND DOMINICKER MULES,
> GONNA TAKE US ON THE OTHER SIDE OF JORDAN.
>
> OH, PULL OFF YOUR OVERCOAT AND ROLL UP YOUR SLEEVES,
> JORDAN IS A HARD ROAD TO TRAVEL;
> PULL OFF YOUR OVERCOAT AND ROLL UP YOUR SLEEVES,
> JORDAN IS A HARD ROAD TO TRAVEL, I BELIEVE.

OLIVE. Now…my favorite song… *(smiles at* **JINKS** *devilishly, then sings the opening words of "Dixie")*
OH, I WISH I WAS IN THE LAND OF COTTON…

JINKS. Oh, no you don't!

EMMA. I don't care for it either, but a promise is a promise.

(Reluctantly, **JINKS** *steps to the mike and a delighted* **OLIVE** *who resumes singing.)*

"DIXIE"

OLIVE.
O, I WISH I WAS IN THE LAND OF COTTON …

JINKS. *(reluctantly joins in song, although without enthusiasm)*
OLD TIMES THERE ARE NOT FORGOTTEN.
LOOK AWAY! LOOK AWAY!
LOOK AWAY! DIXIE LAND.

OLIVE & JINKS. *(together, eventually singing up a storm)*
IN DIXIE LAND WHERE I WAS BORN IN
EARLY ON ONE FROSTY MORN'.
LOOK AWAY! LOOK AWAY!
LOOK AWAY! *DIXIE LAND!*

*(***CORDELIA** *and* **EMMA** *applaud as* **JINKS** *and* **OLIVE** *conclude their song, in part because a bevy of lights – coming from the parking lot – have illuminated the inside of Old Smokey.)*

JINKS. *(pointing out, toward the audience)* Look out there…

CORDELIA. The road…it must've opened…

(All rush to the porch, look out. **CORDELIA** *– the mike in hand – makes sure what's said is broadcasted.)*

Ladies and Gentlemen…our parking lot's almost full…

EMMA. With more cars coming…

OLIVE. Their headlights shining like…

EMMA. Like "Saturday Night At Old Smokey"!

CORDELIA. Look out there, Miz Wilkins…the South is doing it again…everybody's coming together. They're telling us traditions are worth preserving…

EMMA. Like family…

TAMMY. Especially Mamas…

CORDELIA. Country music…

JINKS. *(still not convinced)* Fried chicken…

OLIVE. Old Smokey…

EMMA. *(looking at* **OLIVE** *and* **JINKS**) And old friends! All this happening, we can't be as awful as you've told us we are. Isn't that true, Jinks?

JINKS. Maybe not *as* awful.

EMMA. Maybe not awful at all?

JINKS. Maybe.

(**CORDELIA** *looks at the unseen parking lot which is filled, then begins to clap and sing a song that reflects what she believes East Tennessee is doing [again to the tune of "She'll Be Comin' 'Round The Mountain"]. She signals for the others to join her.*)

CORDELIA.
OH…YOU ARE SAVING OLD SMOKEY –

JINKS. *(interjects the words into* **CORDELIA***'s lyrics)*
FOR TEDDY!

CORDELIA.
YES YOU ARE!

ALL.
OH, YOU ARE SAVING OLD SMOKEY, YES YOU ARE!
YOU'VE CALLED YOUR FRIENDS, YOU'VE CALLED YOUR HONEY,
YOU ARE DONATING MONEY.
OH, YOU ARE SAVING OLD SMOKEY, YES YOU ARE!

CORDELIA & EMMA. *(into the microphone and to those out front, with feeling)*
THANK YOU, EAST TENNESSEE!

(**CORDELIA** *throws a kiss to the audience, after which she,* **TAMMY**, **JINKS** *and* **OLIVE** *continue to sing and clap and carry on in a grand celebration. As they do,*

(EMMA *looks heavenward, perhaps saying a silent, "Thank you." The lights – except those supposedly coming from the parking lot – slowly dim to black. After a moment, they too go to black.*)

End of Play

PROPERTY LIST

Vintage Advertising Signs, perhaps including one reading,
"You Want it, We Sell It" (followed by an illustration of crossed fingers)
Brooms (3)
Mop and Bucket
Dust Cloths
Table Radio
Flashlights (2)
Bowl of Dip With Crackers
Shopping Bag
Three Aprons (two reading "Old Smokey, a third reading "Queen of the South")
Paper Towels
Large Cardboard Box (3)
Smaller Cardboard Box
Several Jars and/or Package of Food Products
A Bouquet of Flowers
Upright Microphone (labeled "WRET" if possible)
Simulated Remote Broadcast Equipment (perhaps nothing more than a laptop computer or something similar, earphones, assorted telephone or electrical cords to seemingly hook various pieces of equipment together)
Sheets of Paper (8-1/2 x 11)
Guitar
A Large Basket
One or More Tambourines
Triangle
Musical Spoons
Washboard
Several Candles (if permitted)
Small Tree Limbs (2)
Checkbook/Check/Pen

SOUND EFFECTS/SPECIAL EFFECTS

Ding-Dong (sound heard at old-time filling stations)
"Dixie" (opening of song played on an automobile-like horn)
Recording of a Song (heard on a radio)
"Amazing Grace!" (recording sung by two female singers)
Ring of a Telephone
Flashes of Lightning
Claps of Thunder
Crashing Sound
Bang and/or Roar Sound
Wind Sounds
Recorded voices for Radio Broadcasts (Cordelia and
WRET's studio announcer – see script)

Also by
Ron Osborne...

First Baptist of Ivy Gap

Ruby's Story

Seeing Stars in Dixie

Showtime at First Baptist

Wise Women

Please visit our website **samuelfrench.com** for complete descriptions and licensing information.

OTHER TITLES AVAILABLE FROM SAMUEL FRENCH

FIRST BAPTIST OF IVY GAP

Ron Osborne

Comedy / 6f / Unit set

During WWII, six women gather at the church to roll bandages and plan the church's 75th anniversary. Overseeing things is Edith, the pastor's wise-cracking wife who dispenses Red Cross smocks and witty repartee to Luby, whose son is fighting in the Pacific; Mae Ellen, the church's rebellious organist who wants to quit but hasn't the courage; Olene, who dreams of a career in Hollywood; Sammy, a shy newcomer with a secret; and Vera, an influential Baptist with a secret of her own. When Luby learns her son has been wounded, she confounds the others by blaming the vulnerable Sammy.

Twenty-five years later, our "First Baptist Six" reunite. Back to reconcile with Luby - whose son died of his wounds - is Sammy, whose own son is now in Vietnam; and Olene, whose flashy show business career will set the town on its ear. There to welcome them are Vera, her secret still safe; Mae Ellen, still rebellious and still looking for an escape; and Edith, whose biggest challenge isn't the church's upcoming centennial but revelations that shake relationships formed over a quarter of a century. With humor and pathos, these six very different women find comfort, forgiveness and redemption in each other. Winner of multiple playwriting awards.

"Will be compared to *Steel Magnolias*, but forget steel; these mountain magnolias are pure gold…humor, drama, warmth and six of the most wonderful characters you'll see - tasty comfort for the playgoer's soul."
– *Bristol Herald-Courier*

"Has drama, tragedy, love, loss and redemption with plenty of comedy too."
– *WhatsHappeningDayton.com*

SAMUELFRENCH.COM

OTHER TITLES AVAILABLE FROM SAMUEL FRENCH

RUBY'S STORY

Ron Osborne

Drama / 3m, 6f / Multiple Sets

June 1944. In England, Allied troops are massing for an invasion. On a small farm in Appalachia, a different kind of war is about to rage. Here, Walter and Grace share a home with four daughters: Rose, who struggles to understand why Stan – an immigrant coal miner and the love of her life – abruptly left to join the Polish Free Forces; Helga, who fears for her husband who's in the Army and – like Stan – assigned to a combat unit in England; Frieda, the family's adventure-seeking daughter, who works in a factory making uniforms and new friends, one of whom she can't bring home; and teenage Ruby who yearns to be the next Edward R. Murrow, but who must first come to grips with a family falling apart at the seams. D-Day speeds the dissolution process. But at its core is Walter's seeming allegiance to his German heritage, no matter that Helga's husband and Rose's fiancé are at war against all things German. There – through every battle – is Grace, hoping liberal doses of humor, love and understanding can restore harmony. It is adult Ruby – back for a funeral, seeking answers to questions that haunt her – who retells the family's struggle against prejudice, fear, delusion and self-loathing.

SAMUELFRENCH.COM

OTHER TITLES AVAILABLE FROM SAMUEL FRENCH

SEEING STARS IN DIXIE

Ron Osborne

Dramatic Comedy / 1m, 4f / Interior

It's 1956 and Hollywood has arrived in Natchez, Mississippi with its brightest stars to film Raintree County. Meanwhile at Clemmie's, a Natchez tea room, the widowed proprietor who has a fascination with movies and a secret admirer, oversees her own cast of characters: Tootie, her take charge friend; Jo Beth, a former beauty queen; Glease, a man more comfortable with women than macho men, and Marjorie, an unethical social climber. Competition for a small role in the movie brings out the best and worst of these memorable characters. Twists, turns and revelations lead Clemmie to trade a moment of fame for love and the chance to impact the lives of people dear to her. Originally produced at the Sonoma County Repertory Theatre in Sebastopol, CA.

"A warm, funny play…hilarious, heart-warming, sassy Southern comedy…a standing ovation."
– *Asheville Citizen-Times*

"Offers jolly good fun…tightly crafted dialogue delivers a chuckle a minute."
– *Starkville Daily News*

SAMUELFRENCH.COM

OTHER TITLES AVAILABLE FROM SAMUEL FRENCH

SHOWTIME AT FIRST BAPTIST

Ron Osborne

Dramatic Comedy / 6f

Showtime at First Baptist is the sequel to the hugely popular and widely produced *First Baptist of Ivy Gap*.

First Baptist of Ivy Gap's 100th anniversary picnic was a smashing success, except for one little thing: the bolt of lightning that struck the church's steeple, igniting a fire that destroyed the sanctuary and so much more. In the wake of the disaster, key women of the church – led by Edith, the pastor's take-charge wife – gather in what's left (the fellowship hall) to commiserate and try to put things back together. To raise spirits and funds for rebuilding, the women plan an evening of entertainment designed to showcase the congregation's talent. Could it be that some of Edith's gang plan a song and dance number that may shock the congregation? If so, how will they circumvent the authority of the all-male conservative board of deacons, not to mention, one of their own? Change is in the air as these six diverse women challenge institutions as well as each other. Along the way, there are laughs to be shared, battles to be fought, love to be won, relationships to be mended, and losses to be grieved. >

"Good natured religious jokes aplenty and drama…But the real meat is a gentle, warm story about six good women and how they came together despite times that are, 'a changing' …A serious play and a delightful comedy…I sure enjoyed it." – *Bristol Herald-Courier*

"Sure to be an instant classic…This touching comedy is full of laughs, realistic characters and thought-provoking issues…The Southern women who inhabit the world of Ivy Gap are amazing! Osborne can definitely write great women characters…It's small-town politics at its most entertaining…Bring the whole family."
– *Washington County News*

SAMUELFRENCH.COM

OTHER TITLES AVAILABLE FROM SAMUEL FRENCH

WISE WOMEN

Ron Osborne

Comedy / 2m, 4f / Unit set

It's almost Christmas, 1944. In Knoxville, Tennessee, a frustrated mother with a secret and a teenage daughter with a dream take in two young roomers who work at a nearby bomb-making plant. Both girls are asserting their independence, one in the company of servicemen, the other as a contestant in a Miss Bombshell U.S.A. competition, an action that puts her at odds with her father, a preacher in a small Virginia town. Along the way, the teenage daughter, who worries more about rumors of an asteroid said to be streaking toward nearby Chattanooga than a vicious war raging around the world, bamboozles her mother into allowing her to attend a Frank Sinatra concert at the local USO. When she brings home a young war-bound Marine as naive as herself, this colorful collection of characters is pulled apart, then mended with humor, romance, twists, turns and revelations. As these women struggle, grow and ultimately succeed, at least for one fragile moment in time-they remind us that we're all "family" and, in each other's company, we may find ourselves.

"*Wise Women* offers holiday warmth, laughs…moving and funny."
– *The Bristol Herald-Courier*

"A charming, bittersweet comedy…a strong work for
the holiday season."
– *Washington County News*

"Lively and believable characters in a delightful spicy-sweet story."
– *Johnson City Press*

SAMUELFRENCH.COM

www.ingramcontent.com/pod-product-compliance
Lightning Source LLC
Chambersburg PA
CBHW070646300426
44111CB00013B/2285